The Decorative Arts of the FORTIES and FIFTIES

AUSTERITY Binge

Bevis Hillier

The Decorative Arts of the FORTIES and FIFTIES

AUSTERITY Binge

Bevis Hillier

 Clarkson N. Potter, Inc./Publisher NEW YORK
Distributed by Crown Publishers, Inc.

Acknowledgements
Acknowledgements are gratefully made to the following for permission to quote : B. T. Batsford Ltd for the extract from *Night Thoughts of a Country Landlady* (p. 14) ; John Pudney for 'Civilized Man' © John Pudney 1942 (p. 15) ; Cassell & Co. for *The Camouflage Story* (p. 41) ; Sir George Weidenfeld for the extracts from *Contact* (pp. 50, 51, and 77) ; Faber & Faber for 'The Dowser' (p. 63) and 'Elvis Presley' (p. 168) ; Oxford University Press, New York for 'The Dowser' (p. 63) ; Penguin Books Ltd for *Popular Art in the United States* (p. 79) ; Penguin Books Ltd and Farrar, Straus & Giroux Inc. for *London War Notes* (p. 38) ; Jonathan Cape Ltd and Harold Matson Co. Inc. for 'Pegasus' (p. 91) ; J. M. Dent & Sons Ltd and E. P. Dutton and Co. Inc. for *Shocking Life* (pp. 96 and 134) ; Edith Pargeter for *Lost Children* (pp. 110–13) ; the Executors of Dorothy Wellesley for *Lost Planet and Other Poems* (p. 159) ; Hodder & Stoughton Ltd and A. D. Peters & Co. for *Age of Austerity* (p. 167) ; *Life* Magazine for 'The Nifty Fifties', © 1972 Time Inc. (p. 192) and United Artists for 'American Pie' (p. 189).

Library of Congress Catalog Card Number : 74-83243

Inquiries should be addressed to Clarkson N. Potter, Inc., 419 Park Avenue South, New York, N.Y. 10016

First American Edition published in 1975 by Clarkson N. Potter, Inc.

Printed and bound in Holland by Callenbach b.v., Nijkerk

Contents

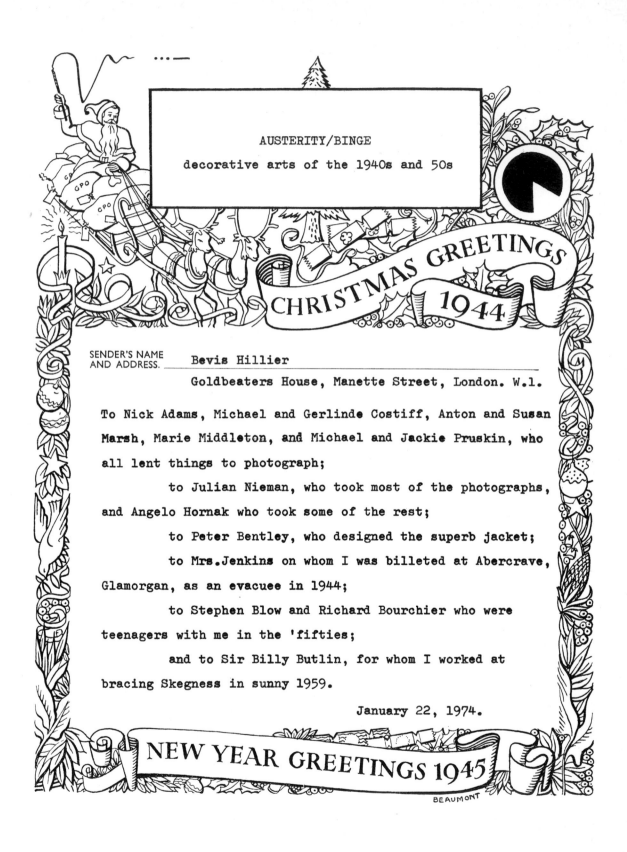

AUSTERITY/BINGE

decorative arts of the 1940s and 50s

CHRISTMAS GREETINGS 1944

SENDER'S NAME AND ADDRESS. **Bevis Hillier**

Goldbeaters House, Manette Street, London. W.1.

To Nick Adams, Michael and Gerlinde Costiff, Anton and Susan Marsh, Marie Middleton, and Michael and Jackie Pruskin, who all lent things to photograph;

to Julian Nieman, who took most of the photographs, and Angelo Hornak who took some of the rest;

to Peter Bentley, who designed the superb jacket;

to Mrs.Jenkins on whom I was billeted at Abercrave, Glamorgan, as an evacuee in 1944;

to Stephen Blow and Richard Bourchier who were teenagers with me in the 'fifties;

and to Sir Billy Butlin, for whom I worked at bracing Skegness in sunny 1959.

January 22, 1974.

NEW YEAR GREETINGS 1945

BEAUMONT

Hearing one saga, we enact the next.
We please our elders when we sit enthralled ;
But then they're puzzled ; and at last they're vexed
To have their youth so avidly recalled.

It dawns upon the veterans after all
That what for them were agonies, for us
Are high-brow thrillers, though historical ;
And all their feats quite strictly fabulous.

Donald Davie

Foreword by Sir John Betjeman

The sage Max Beerbohm remarked that a man must be mad to take himself *quite* seriously. How true the pages of this book prove his saying to be. Bevis Hillier, who compiled it and wrote the sprightly and well-informed text, also, I like to think, had a hand in the layout of the pages, choosing which picture to show opposite which and what sort of a mad border to give to the letter press. Great thought and care have gone to this alarming selection.

Ted McKnight Kauffer, whose posters electrified London of the thirties – you will remember the crowing cock for Enos Fruit Salt and his underground pictures for Frank Pick and Shell posters for Jack Beddington – once said to me when I asked him about the new romantic, representational paintings by John Piper, 'He has an exciting eye.' Bevis Hillier also has an exciting eye. I don't see how anyone looking through these pages can fail to be diverted nor become too solemn.

The struggle out of war propaganda in the forties, pin-ups, ration cards and camouflage and then the return to nature itself by barge and caravan and circus tents. The craze for mermaids, flying horses and later for flying saucers, light-hearted heraldry, neo-Regency, and then, like a new broom, the Festival of Britain in 1951, leaving the South Bank swept of wharfs and instead dominated by the Festival Hall whose river front undoubtedly looks like an outsize television set (see page 131). In all these sweepings, Bevis Hillier has kept a sense of proportion and excitement. 'What are we going to come to next? Oh yes, I remember that.' Every page is a surprise.

The single issue of a periodical is always more interesting than the bound volume. The advertisement pages show the standard of popular taste. In this book advertisements predominate. The chief sources of supply for ideas and styles of art have been advertising agents whose profession it is to be trendy.

Different generations will react in different ways to this book. I was brought up to admire Liberty silks and Japanese art and unstained oak. In fact, quietness was taste and noise was vulgarity. What shocks and shouts must Bevis Hillier have braved! What catalogues and trade supplements must his comprehensive mind have scanned to complete this dazzling portrait of those two decades! For here we are in all our pathos and pretentiousness.

Introduction

And what happened *then*, Daddy? As I had written two books on Art Deco[1] – the decorative arts of the 1920s and 30s – it was a natural progression to want to study Austerity/Binge – the decorative arts of the 1940s and 50s. Some people find the idea of such an exercise ridiculous. When I edited for the London *Sunday Times* a series on 'antiques' which ended with the period 1920–40, the satirical magazine *Private Eye* thought it a huge joke to parody the series with a spoof feature on the period 1940–50, including an electric toaster, an Exide battery, a mangle, a Parker Quink bottle ('The label is considered to be a masterpiece of 40s graphics'), and 'an upholstered armchair by Bevis Hillier. Hillier was a founder member of the Tottenham Court Road School and this chair with its imaginative use of coil springs and heavy oak frame is considered by many critics to be an ideal way of starting a bonfire. Oak leaf motif by Daphne du Youmindlov harks back to Beloff, Plinth, Hoggmeyer, Bondalini, Mopz, Nagasaki and Meinzadoppel-diamond-Vatvevantisvatnis. £890.'

A study of Austerity/Binge is open to two main objections. First, that the period is too recent for an objective assessment. Secondly, that too little of real quality came out of the period to make it worth writing about. The first objection would deprive us of Ptolemy's memoirs of Alexander the Great, or Bede's account of the great churchmen he remembered, or the writings of any historian who can say *Et quorum pars parva fui.*[2] Again, someone who is twenty-one now was born when the period under review (1940–60) had already run more than half its course. To such a person, the 1940s and most of the 1950s are as arcane historically, are as much 'past history', as the Royalist *v.* Puritan Civil War; indeed, young men today may find it easier to identify with Hyacinthine-locked cavaliers of the 1640s than with short-back-and-sides warriors of the 1940s. From the collector's point of view, collecting Austerity/Binge is both easier and cheaper now than it will be in, say twenty years' time; and this early interest in forties and fifties relics may preserve many that would otherwise be thrown away or allowed to deteriorate. Besides, the forties and fifties are already the subject of an enthusiastic and wide-ranging revival (see pp. 184-196); and when a period is ripe for nostalgia – which is history by spontaneous combustion – it is probably ready for the historian too.

To the second objection, that there is too little of quality from the period to be worth considering, there are three answers. First, that as no one has yet given the decorative art of the period serious consideration, the best works may not yet all have come to light (just as, with Art Deco, although Ruhlmann and Puiforcat were recognized from the outset of the revival as masters, it took some time to establish who were the rest of the élite). Secondly, that the designers of real genius to whom I direct attention in this book – for example, the marvellously original Italian furniture designers, Mollino, Buffa, Chiesa, Rava and Pestalozza – are impressive enough to deserve a book to themselves. Thirdly, and by far the most important, I believe that the decorative arts of *any* period are worth considering, however barren of talent they may seem to be or may in fact be – provided that the writer attempts to interpret them in social as well as aesthetic terms. To ignore a period of decorative art because the materials available in the austerity during and after a terrible war were limited, or because the fine flower of young artists had fallen in battle, or because the themes that obsessed bomb-haunted and peace-yearning minds were in some ways different from those which possess ours, is as fatuously arrogant as to despise or ignore some part of society which, from poverty or other cause, is different from one's own. This is not a communist theory of art history, but simply a humanitarian one.

In the preface to my first Art Deco book I stated that my aim was the exact opposite of Professor Gombrich's in *The Story of Art,* which he said was 'to limit myself to real works of art, and cut out anything which might merely be interesting as a specimen of taste or fashion'. Here, as there, I will be frequently concerned with what Panofsky called iconology – the study of artistic motifs and developments in relation to contemporary culture at large.

Why 'Austerity/Binge'? In England, the period begins with wartime austerity and continues with it up to and including the 'You've never had it so good' of the late 1950s; but for the Americans (who became so dominant an influence in Britain in the 1950s) it was less a period of austerity. At least the Americans were affluent enough to pack up 'Bundles for Britain'. When I asked an American dealer friend what they had called the period immediately after the war, he replied 'We called it the Binge' – a fresh-sounding, yet period-slang word which also seemed to me to typify the English 'regeneration' feeling of the 1951 junketings and beyond. I was amused to read in David Niven's autobiography *The Moon's a Balloon* that Montgomery posted just inside his 5 Corps headquarters a large notice reading: 'Are you 100% fit? Are you 100% efficient? Do you have 100% Binge?' Niven writes: 'We never discovered what he meant by ''Binge'' because nobody dared to ask him.'

THE FORTIES

Plastic Brooch with arti-
ficial pearl – 'Remember
Harbor' (Pearl Harbor)
Marie Middleton

13

THE ARTS OF WAR

More than anything else surviving from 1940-60, objects from the war years have usually to be treated as social relics rather than as works of art. When you are waging a war, you have other things to think of than decoration. The change from the garish patterning of late Art Deco to the dun colours of wartime is typified in this passage from Edith Olivier's 1943 book *Night Thoughts of a Country Landlady* (illustrated, with a pre-war flippancy, by Rex Whistler):

> There are two phrases which will be for ever inscribed on the hearts of war-time house-keepers – Shopping Bag and Food Queue . . . It is no use getting into a food queue, or into a bus queue which will land you in one, unless you possess a shopping bag. Without that, you must carry home a miscellaneous collection of onions, cabbages, fish and tea cakes in your pockets, for the salvage minister will not let you have any paper.
>
> So every woman now owns a shopping bag, and she is jealously possessive about it. At first these bags were brilliant and striking-looking objects – in vivid colours and jazz designs; but as the war years roll on, and cleaning materials grow hard to come by, they all decline to the same level of dusty duskiness, reminiscent of two colours fashionable in my youth – Elephant's Breath and Desert Sand.

There were exceptions to the general moratorium on design. Some care was naturally taken over pictorial propaganda; and although the standard of Second World War posters was far lower, in all the combatant countries, than in the Great War[1] – the uninspired American examples shown here represent the average – some masterly designs were produced by Abram Games, and the laconic deftness of Fougasse's 'Careless Talk' posters showed how a deadly serious point could be made memorable through humour. Fougasse was also the designer of the charity book . . . *and the gatepost* (1940), which contained a detachable stamp to stick over the receiver rest of your telephone ('or round the column of your telephone if it is of the ''candlestick'' type') showing Hitler's head and inscribed 'Maybe he's listening too', with the 'Careless talk costs lives' slogan.

Book design was in general as literally down to earth as the jacket for W. E. Shewell-Cooper's *Eating without Heating* or that for G. T. McKenna's *Allotmenteering in Wartime*. But there was really no reason why good design should not go with cheap production, as the admirable jacket for John Pudney's *Dispersal Point and Other Air Poems* (1942) proves. Such defiant quality in a time of shoddiness gave point to the last stanza of Pudney's poem 'Civilized Man' in that volume:

ALAIN MEATH EVANS. •Typographer. Bethlehem Press. London. England

Wartime motto placard issued by the Bethlehem Press, London

Jacket of *Allotmenteering in Wartime* by G. T. McKenna, London 1944

ALLOT ENTEERING
IN WARTIME

G.T. McKENNA

I shall take more killing than you think,
Who think the beautiful lives of men crushed out
In lead, and slime and stink
Of agony and petrol, make a final rout.

It was a heyday for paperback books, which could be posted abroad more easily than hardbacks and served as portable universities and evening classes to men whose education had been cut short. Here too there was some enterprising design; at times, photographic effects replaced the graphics-only of the Art Deco period,[2] as in the cover for a paperback version of Simenon's *Le Voyageur de la Toussaint* (1941) in which a young couple in archetypal forties clothes gaze into the future with an optimism that cannot have seemed very plausible in 1941 France.

'Handy Postals' : postcard book for use of the United States Navy, Second World War

Handy
Postals

UNITED STATES NAVY

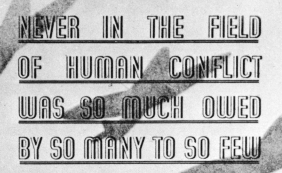

NEVER IN THE FIELD
OF HUMAN CONFLICT
WAS SO MUCH OWED
BY SO MANY TO SO FEW

WINSTON CHURCHILL

BETHLEHEM PRESS, (EVANS-NELSON) TYPOGRAPHERS

Wartime motto placard issued by the Bethlehem Press, London

Propaganda

Although it must appear callous or intolerably flippant to say so, many of the relics of the Second World War which it is possible to collect have a comic or kitsch quality. This is true even of gas masks, with their weird chrysalis-green snouts ('Mickey Mouse' masks for some children[3]) – emblems of anticlimax on a grand scale, of preparation, none too effectual in any case, for an evil which never arrived. Their dual aspects, sinister and ludicrous, had already been exploited before the war by John Heartfield, the great German anti-Nazi master of photomontage,[4] in his 'What the Angels got for Christmas' (1935).

Patriotism produced *The British Boys' and Girls' Wartime Playbook* ('Colour your own barrage-balloon'); *The Happy Gang goes to it,* showing Rover and Mousey ready to take off to intercept Hun bombers; a vase in the form of a hollow 'V' for Victory, on floral base, dated 1942; and 'The Boss', a dogged little figure of Churchill by the Bovey Pottery, Devon, with hollow legs that fit on to the prongs of a special ebonized wood plinth. The Fielding Pottery, Staffordshire, marketed ashtrays in the form of miniature chamber pots. One, with Hitler's face inside, is inscribed: 'Flip your ashes on Old Nasty – Jerry No. 1 – the Violation of Po-land'; the other contains Goering's face, with the legend: 'Flip your

Gasmasks of the Second World War

16

THE BRITISH BOYS AND GIRLS
WARTIME PLAYBOOK
No. 1

A NEW NOVELTY—"PAPER-PAINTING"—WITHOUT USING PAINTS

Cover of *The British Boys' and Girls' Playbook No. 1*

READY TO TAKE OFF

Illustration from *The Happy Gang Goes to It*, a painting book. Valentine and Sons Ltd, Dundee and London

'V for Victory' vase. Incised, 'Sample, A.M. Jan-1942'. Printed, 'Made in England' Height 16 cm (6½ in.) Marie Middleton

Pottery figure of Winston Churchill 'The Boss' by the Bovey Pottery, England, showing special wooden plinth. Height (with plinth) 18 cm (7in.). John and Diana Lyons

Children's puzzle: Put the Yanks in Berlin
USA, Second World War. Made by
Modern Novelties Inc. of 4000 Orange
Avenue, Cleveland, Ohio

ashes on Old Piggy – Jerry No. 2'. Gratitude to our eastern forces produced the 'Paiforce' tankard with trumpeting elephant's head. Jessica Dragonette, the 1930s radio star, central figure of the Art Deco batik mural, 'The History of Radio', by Arthur Gordon Smith,[5] was now with the American war services, selling war bonds. A pamphlet headed with the characteristic script printing of the 1940s showed Jessica Dragonette riding in a jeep and a leopardskin coat; Jessica Dragonette eating with the rookies at Westover Field, Mass.; singing to troops at Brookley Field, Mobile, Alabama; accepting a bouquet at Fort Francis

Songsheet, 'Sweet Dreams,
Sweetheart' from the Warner
Brothers picture *Hollywood
Canteen*, USA 1944

'Good Morning, Miss Kane' from *Terry and the Pirates* coloring book, Saalfied Publishing Company, Akron, Ohio, and New York, Second World War.

'Terry poured too much coffee into his cup' from *Terry and the Pirates* coloring book.

'Oh, Miss Burma, you know so many things', from *Terry and the Pirates* coloring book

'How are you, Charlie?' from *Terry and the Pirates* coloring book

Porcelain ashtray in the form of a miniature chamber-pot, by Fielding's, England. Height 4 cm depth 5 cm (1½ × 2 in.)

'Paiforce' mug, silver-plated, 1945

E. Warren, Cheyenne, Wyoming; standing with Walter Pidgeon in Toronto; selling a bond at the Columbia Broadcasting Studios; and being honoured by the Pope. The most kitsch souvenir of all also came from America: a plastic brooch made up of the script letters 'Remember Harbor', the words divided by an artificial pearl so that the whole message, including rebus, reads: 'Remember Pearl Harbor'. There had perhaps been no commemoration of human suffering more grotesque since the monument at Ancrum, near Selkirk, Scotland, which celebrates the heroine of a Scottish-English battle:

> Fair Maiden Lilliard lies under this stane.
> Little was her stature, but muckle is her fame;
> Upon the English loons she laid mony, mony thumps
> And when her legs were cuttit aff
> She fought upon her stumps.

Public health posters had their funny side. A British poster showed 'The Common Bed Bug', presented square-on for recognition, like the silhouette of a Heinkel or Messerschmidt. 'Don't keep it dark!' the poster advised, conjuring up the vision of a nation of clandestine bed-bug hoarders, living in mortal terror of the prowling sanitary inspector. A health poster torn down as a souvenir in Cairo showed another warning silhouette, this time of a girl with long hair and leg-o'-mutton sleeves against a red light, and with the caption:

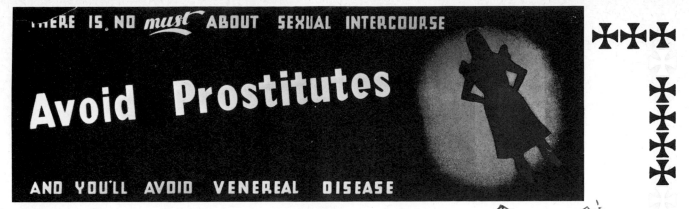

Poster torn down in Cairo, Second World War. The late Major Oliver Woods

There is no *must* about sexual intercourse
Avoid Prostitutes
and you'll avoid venereal disease.

The things that were meant to be funny seem rather less so now : for example, the words of 'Adolf', a song composed, words and music, by Annette Mills. The songsheet cover had a portrait of Arthur Askey inset in a drawing of Hitler being spanked by a tin-hatted Tommy. The words went :

> Adolf, you've bitten off much more than you can chew
> Come on, hold your hand out, we're all fed up with you.
> Adolf, you toddle off, and all your Nazis too,
> Or you may get something to remind you of the Old Red, White and Blue.
>
> (*Cor Blimey*).

Jack Warner's rhymes in the same sheet about Claude and his Sword, and Frank and his Tank, were not much funnier.

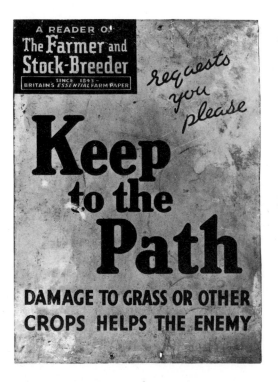

'Keep to the Path' from *The Farmer and Stock Breeder*

Songsheet of 'Adolf' by Annette Mills

Advertisement for 'Vimms' vitamin tablets, *Redbook Magazine*, New York, June 1943

Advertisement for Utility furniture in *Everybody's*, 8 April 1944

UTILITY

Bedstead with Wire Spring
£4.3.9 cash **or ON OUR**
EASY TERMS

Get it at . . .

The Times

FURNISHING CO.

235-238, HIGH HOLBORN, W.C.1

BRANCHES ALL OVER ENGLAND

LINOLEUM Our supplies of felt base linoleum will be reserved for holders of Utility Furniture Permits.

FOOD RATIONING SURE HAD ME WORRIED

"**With shortages** it's hard to get enough vitamin-rich foods. Yet I didn't want my family to get tired, low in resistance . . . vitamin-deficient. That started me thinking. Vimms, I found, have all the essential vitamins and all the minerals commonly lacking. And they require no points at all!

SEE WHAT 3 VIMMS A DAY SUPPLY

Vitamin A as much as in 20 pats BUTTER	Vitamin B₁ as much as in ¾ lb. cooked LIVER	Vitamin B₂ (G) as much as in ⅞ QUART MILK
Vitamin C as much as in 5 oz. TOMATO JUICE	Vitamin D as much as in 2 tsp. COD LIVER OIL	Vitamin P-P (Niacin Amide) as much as in ⅓ lb. STEAK
CALCIUM as much as in 1½ oz. AMER. CHEESE	PHOSPHORUS as much as in 1½ EGGS	IRON as much as in 2 cups SPINACH

"**This gives you an idea** of what Vimms supply. They fit right into any modern plan of family feeding. Vimms are pleasant to take, too. And they meet two simple rules of vitamin buying:

1. They give you all the vitamins Government experts say are essential
2. They give them to you in the balanced formula doctors endorse

In addition, Vimms give you *all* the minerals commonly lacking.

SURRENDER OR ELSE!

NO VITAMIN SHORTAGE IN MY FAMILY, THANKS TO **VIMMS**

"'**Get that Vimms feeling**' used to be just a slogan to me. But my youngsters sure have got it now. I must have needed extra vitamins too, because I feel a lot better myself. Why don't you try Vimms? They cost only a nickel a day in the Family Size." At your druggist's. Lever Brothers Company, Pharmaceutical Div., Cambridge, Mass.

All the vitamins known to be essential and all the minerals commonly lacking.
24 tablets 50¢; 96 tablets $1.75; 288 tablets $5.00

Keeping up Morale in the Village Hall by Gluck, 1944

Souvenir of liberation, Belgium, 1944, drawn by Ebinger, Antwerp

Opposing headscarfs: Italian fascist scarf with 'Duce' and fasces motifs; scarf with RAF symbol and Churchill quotations Vernon Lambert

Programme of Frank Semmes' Moulin Rouge,
Hollywood. 1950s

Too tired to sleep

.... Take a QUICK warm bath (body temperature). Hop into bed.

and THEN—Lie on your side with body curled up as small as you can make it. Begin uncurling by pushing down with the feet and up with the arms and head until you've stretched with your whole body as far as you can. Roll on to your back and relax. Repeat two or three times on each side.

NOW—Lie flat on your back with arms stretched over the head. Lift your right hip—relax. Lift your left shoulder—relax. Repeat same with the left hip and right shoulder. Be sure that when you lift your shoulders, hips remain flat, and when you lift your hips, shoulders remain flat. Repeat four or five times.

One more stretch .... as hard as you can. And then relax!

Finally: Breathe a little deeper than usual for a few minutes and then *HAPPY DREAMS.*

The tempo and tension of the jobs we are doing plus the strain of the world in which we're living make it imperative for all of us to know how to relax. But we can't leave relaxing to chance. We must make a conscious effort to relieve our bodies of the strains and tensions that accumulate. To consciously relax, use the exercises and suggestions given here. They will do wonders for you. Lay greatest stress on those exercises and suggestions that apply specifically to your individual aches and "weak spots." In addition to the proper conscious relaxation, we urge a periodic medical check up and adequate food, rest, recreation and hygienic practices. The sum total will help to keep you feeling up to the job you're doing.

RELAX AT HOME—WORK
BETTER ON THE JOB.

Material prepared by the Staff of the Office of Physical Fitness, New York State War Council

Illustrations by: SUZY PERLMAN

For further information on the Industrial Fitness Program address:

DR. HIRAM A. JONES, *Director*
Office of Physical Fitness
New York State War Council
State Education Building
Albany 1, New York

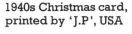

OFFICE OF PHYSICAL FITNESS
NEW YORK STATE WAR COUNCIL

'Relax at home: work better on the
job' issued by the Office of Physical
Fitness, New York State War Council,
Second World War.

1940s Christmas card,
printed by 'J.P', USA

24

"*Dear Gertrood*"

Title page of *Dear Gertrood* by Wendell Ehret, published by Robert McBride & Company, New York, 1945

'Plymouth is the 1940 Beauty'. Advertisement in *Life* magazine, 23 October 1939

Bronze, *Genius des Sieges*
by Adolf Wamper, Berlin
1940

Nazi propaganda art[6] in Germany included the Herrenvolk statues by Arno Breker (the officially most approved sculptor), Adolf Wamper, Fritz Behn, Georg Kolbe and Milly Steger, with the aged Maillol co-opted; schmaltzy paintings of traditional folk Austria by Sepp Hilz, idealized portraits of Hitler and the SS, the pallid neo-classicism of Adolf Ziegler and Georg Friedrich, and the more erotic mythology of M. Paul Padua. Mosaic, as a medium of heroic antiquity, was in favour for the decoration of buildings: August Wagner of the Vereinigte Werkstätten für Mosaik und Glasmalerei (United workshops for mosaic and glass-painting), Berlin-Treptow, executed suitably uplifting designs for the State Chancery, the Conference Hall of the Deutsches Museum, Munich, (both designed by Professor Hermann Kaspar of Munich), the Temple of Honour, Munich (designed by Wilhelm Putz, Munich), the Hall of Pillars at the National Party Conference Building, Nuremberg (designed by Kaspar), the main post office, Stuttgart (designed by R. Yelin, Stuttgart) and the General Goering Barracks, Berlin (designed by Hans Uhl, Berlin). Nazi emblems were also carved and painted on ordinary household furniture; one imagines there is little left of it today. Anti-Nazi art, in the tradition of Grosz, Heartfield and Lynd Ward, is represented here by two of the illustrations from L. J. Jordaan's 1945 contribution to *De Groene,* Amsterdam.

Marble mosaic in the entrance to the main post office, Stuttgart. Designed by R. Yelin, Stuttgart. Executed by August Wagner, Vereinigte Werkstatten fur Mosaik und Glasmalerei, Berlin-Treptow.

Larch wardrobe carved with swastika and Nazi slogans

Chest carved with swastika emblem

Anti-Nazi cartoon by L. J. Jordaan, *De Groene*, 1945

Anti-Nazi cartoon by L. J. Jordaan, *De Groene*, 1945

Pin-ups

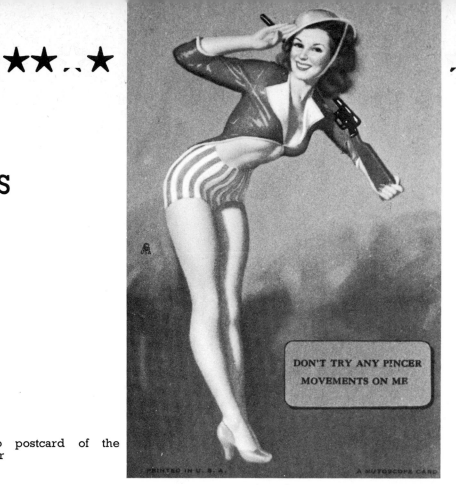

DON'T TRY ANY PINCER
MOVEMENTS ON ME

American pin-up postcard of the
Second World War

A more appealing form of war art was the pin-up. The most popular pin-up girl was Betty Grable, with her famous legs insured for a million dollars; in 1944 she starred in a film called *Pin-Up Girl.* Early in 1941 the Petty Girl – the 1940s equivalent of the Gibson Girl of the turn of the century, and like her named after her creator, in this case George Petty – began to appear in the foldout pages of *Esquire.* From October 1940 she had a rival in the Varga Girl drawn by Alberto Vargas, and in December 1940 the first Varga Girl calendar was issued. An article of 1945 on 'The "pin up" craze among G.I.s' recorded that:

> Crews of the U.S.A.A.F. often plaster the centre sections of Flying Fortresses with drawings and photographs clipped from the pages of *Esquire, Men Only, Look,* and similar publications. One navigator had most of the film stars, including Gypsy Rose Lee, accompanying him on day trips to Berlin, and, in his enthusiasm, had pasted his pin ups on both the inside and the outside of his Fortress. On each flight down the 'Kraut Run', the Navigator's skipper swore that their particular plane was singled out for special attention by the German fighter pilots who 'wondered what all the queer pictures were about.'[7]

Pin-ups became big business, and remained so after the war. An article by Fay Vickers in *Photo World* of August 1946, 'The Great American Pin-up', said:

> This form of art has found its way from the fox-hole to the home. Psychologists say there is no harm in it. . . .
>   In America, vast organizations exist to cater for the pin-up fans. Bob Harrison, of New York City, is one well-known magnate of this type of business. He runs a thriving publishing concern almost entirely devoted to the picturization of subjects for interior decoration. This modern maestro of the pin-up cult has, like Ziegfeld, dedicated his life to the glorification of American womanhood in its full, and sometimes over-ripe, bloom. From his editorial offices spring magazines entitled *Wink, Eyeful,* and *Beauty Parade,* all of which promise 'gals, gags, giggles.' Chiefly responsible for each week's

Jessica Dragonette with the war services,
USA, Second World War

Jessica Dragonette, 'America's Beloved
Sweetheart', at the Ford Summer Hour, 1940

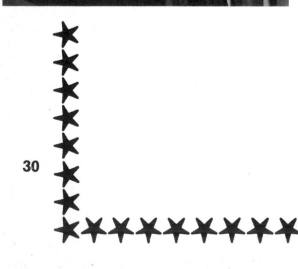

30

CORDET BAG No. 4801

CORDET BAG No. 4810

KORDETTE BAG No. 4815

Jack Frost
HANDBAGS

Cover and three plates from 'Jack Frost
Handbags', USA 1945

GIMP BAG NO. 4810
INSTRUCTIONS ON PAGE 4

VOLUME 48
PRICE 20¢

Advertisement for Beech-Nut Gum,
Cosmopolitan (USA) September 1943

Cover of *The War Illustrated* 28th March, 1941,
with portrait of F. D. Roosevelt

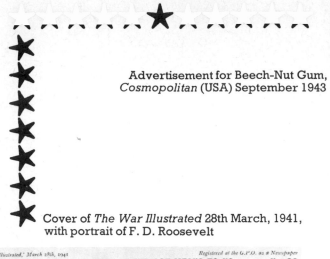

quota of gals is Edythe Farrell, editor and skilled pin-up picker for the Harrison organization. . . . It is not enough merely to photograph a beautiful girl wearing only a bra', panties and a warm smile. Behind every pin-up there must be an idea. Miss Farrell has plenty of ideas and specializes in thinking up adequate reasons for inadequacy of dress.

The Esquire Girls (starting April 1946) were joined in the early fifties by *Esquire's* Lady Fair series, and in 1953 by *Playboy* magazine.

Leonora K. Green, *A Week's Rations for Two*, signed and dated 1941. Private
collection

Gluck, *Soldiers in the NAAFI*, 1944. Fine Art Society

Cover of record album, Irving Berlin's *This is the Army*

Headscarf issued at Camp Pickett, Virginia, Second World War. Vernon Lambert

Fine Art Society *Opposite* Margaret Gere (1878-1965), *Partings at Paddington*, 194

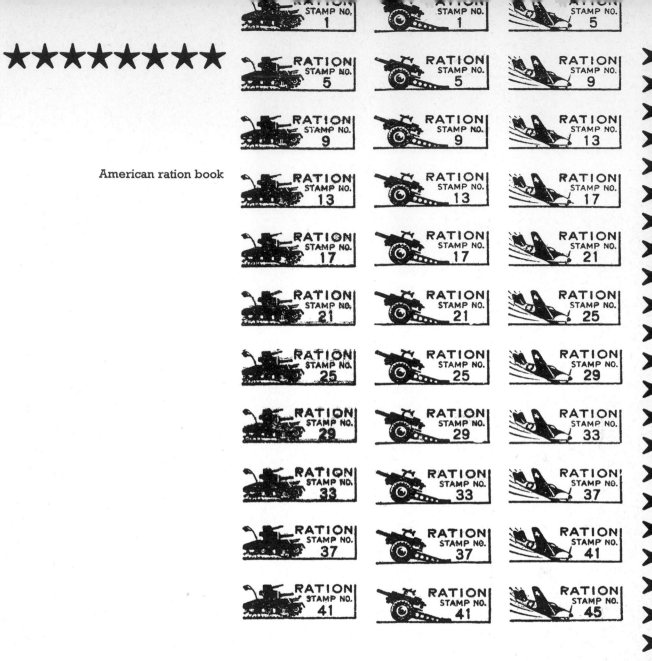

★★★★★★★

American ration book

Staff car, USA, Second World War.
Made by Louis Marx

"SOME CHICKEN—
SOME NECK!"

WINSTON CHURCHILL

Bethlehem Press (Jimmy, Typographer)

Wartime motto placard issued by the Bethlehem Press, London

Camouflage

Propaganda and pin-ups were art forms directly produced by war, but certain aspects of war affected design more indirectly. One of these was camouflage. When seeking for a reason why amoeba-like shapes had invaded design in the second half of the forties – as in an Alvar Aalto glass vase of 1947, a Jacqueline Groag textile design for Hill Brown in 1948, a furnishing fabric named 'Poison' designed by Josef Frank for Svensk Tenn also in '48, or a plywood table designed by Carl-Axel Acking for A. B. Svenska Mobelfabrikerna in 1949 – my first thought was that the influence was the wooden reliefs of Jean Arp, which were certainly popular in the forties and which often include the amoeboid motifs which might be called, by fair use of oxymoron, 'amorphous shapes'. But then I met Julian Trevelyan, one of the many artists who had been involved in camouflage work during the war, and he told me that they had used the term 'wigglies' for the amoeboid shapes painted to conceal targets. Mollie Panter-Downes told her American readers on 27 January 1940 :

> Quite a number of well-known artists are doing camouflage work in various parts of the British Isles. The other day, one of them asked for permission from the Air Ministry to go up in a plane and take a peek at his handiwork, remarking that it was impossible to get any idea of its efficacy from the ground, and after a good deal of waiting about, the request was granted. The camouflage artist hurried aloft with a pilot, but before he even had time to pop his head over the side, so the story goes, there was a roar of shrapnel bursting around the plane and the two men found themselves making a hasty forced landing, badly scared, and quite a bit damaged, in a field in Essex. No one, it seems, had passed on word of the flight to the men in charge of a nearby anti-aircraft battery, who gleefully scampered to gun stations and let fly when spotters reported an unidentified plane approaching.[8]

Cover of the catalogue for the Arp exhibition, Valentin Gallery, New York 1949

Jean Royere, room design, Paris 1946

Glass flower vase by Alvar Aalto 1947

39

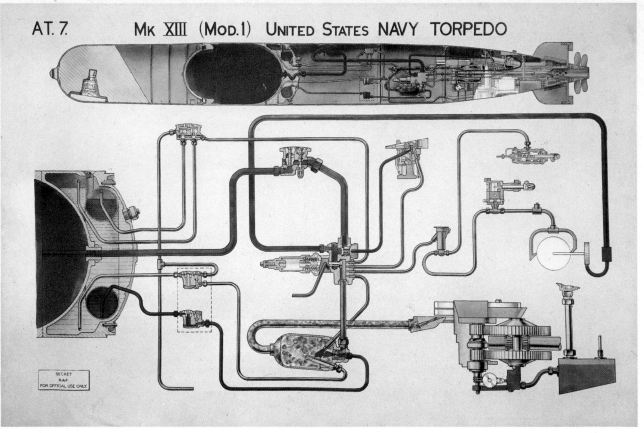

AT. 7.   Mk XIII (Mod.1) United States NAVY TORPEDO

SECRET
R.A.F.
FOR OFFICIAL USE ONLY.

Design of the United States Navy Torpedo, Mk xiii (Mod. 1), Second World War.

Large terracotta model of a mermaid, partially glazed, anon., c. 1947, 56 × 56 × 20 cm, (20 × 20 × 8 in). Mr and Mrs Lewis V. Winter, New York

Among those involved in camouflage work were Oliver Messel,[9] the theatre and ballet designer, James Gardner, who in 1946 was to design the 'Britain Can Make It' exhibition,[10] Basil Spence, and the wood-engraver Blair Hughes-Stanton.[11] The latter was in a group led by Lieutenant-Colonel Geoffrey Barkas,[12] who, as Director of Camouflage with Middle East Forces, created and led the camouflage organization in that theatre from the beginning on New Year's Day, 1941 – when its total strength was four officers and a half share in a trestle table – to the end. After the brilliant success at Alamein, he returned, in the delightful phrase of his publisher's blurb, 'to fill a camouflage appointment at the War Office', and subsequently resumed his proper trade as a film-maker. Barkas was the kind of man Montgomery often attracted – the wag who gets things done. It was he who sent out, to the bemusement but eventually chuckling approval of the 'brass', this instructional poem on the merits of camouflage :

> Driver George Nathaniel Glover
> Scorned the use of Natural Cover
> And never, never could be made
> To Park his Lorry in the Shade.
> In fact his favourite parking places
> Were Vast and Treeless Open Spaces.
>
> When any of his pals demurred,
> George gave them all a frightful bird.
> Descending from the driver's seat,
> And using words one can't repeat,
> He'd broadcast to the world at large
> His Curious Views on Camouflage.
>
> He would remark, 'Cor strike me pink,
> You must be barmy if you think
> There's any need to hide this bus –
> The whole idea's preposterous.
> Listen, you windy lot of Slobs –
> You see these Greeny-Browny Blobs ?
> Well, that's a special kind of Paint
> That makes things look like What They Ain't.
> No fooling, it's the latest thing –
> It's called Disruptured Patterning.'

The poem is much longer, and of course winds to a grim, inexorable conclusion : because George Nathaniel Glover relies only on 'disruptured patterning' (wigglies) and 'ungarnished nets', the Germans

> landed several tons of Muck
> Right on the top of George's Truck.
>
> Emerging later, safe and sound,
> His comrades searched for miles around
> But Not One Trace did they discover
> Of Driver George Nathaniel Glover.
> And I am also very sorry
> To say they never found his Lorry.

It is disheartening to consider oneself an art historian and to formulate terms such as 'amoeboid' and 'amorphous shapes', only to learn that the War Office long since invented the canonical phrase for the phenomenon. *Disruptured Patterning,* ah !

Picture frame design on cover of
Punch summer number, 1948

Picture-frame design in publicity
handout for Noel Coward's film
Brief Encounter 1946

Frames

Advertisement for 'Evening in Paris' perfume by Bourjois. Redbrook Magazine, USA, June 1943

Advertisement for Sobell Radio. *Photo World*, October 1946

's the ?nd. year that counts

...adios don't usually go wrong but ...mes after the first year little ...may develop in the average set. ... Radio is better than average ...e makers have no hesitation in ...a full TWO YEARS' guarantee ...every set. If anything should ...attention a Sobell engineer will ...job in your own home, entirely ...any cost. ...Sobell gives you this unique ...N Radio Service. Ask your ... to arrange a demonstration.

OBELL
DIO

SERVICE IN THE HOME

Sobell Industries Ltd.,
Langley Park, Bucks.

Spell "IT" to the Marine

With Your
Evening in Paris Make-up

The marines *love* trouble . . . and this exquisite make-up, perfumed with the Fragrance of Romance, can spell heart-trouble in any man's language!

Evening in Paris face powder to create a misty veil of beauty . . . delicate flush of feathery rouge . . . bright accent of Evening in Paris lipstick . . . surely this is a loveliness combination to storm the heart of the most devil-may-care hero!

Face Powder, $1.00 **Lipstick,** 50c ● **Rouge,** 50c ● **Perfume,** $1.25 to $10.00
(All prices plus tax)

Evening in Paris

Distributed by
BOURJOIS

Listen to the new Bourjois radio show, "Here's to Romance" with David Broekman's orchestra, the songs of Buddy Clark and Jim Ameche as Master of Ceremonies, Sundays over the Blue Network.

Another motif that war indirectly introduced was the picture frame. The fashion for Victoriana may have had something to do with it, but it is more likely that the wartime habit of separated people communicating through photographs accustomed them to thinking of people and scenes within frames. Many women saw more of their husbands in photograph frames than in bed during the war. One woman whose husband served in the RAF told me that the photo of her husband 'looked horribly like the photographs widows kept on the mantlepiece'. Such a photograph is drawn in an American advertisement of 1943 for Evening in Paris cosmetics ('Spell "IT" to the Marine'). Mothers who would never have wasted money on such vanities in peacetime hauled their children down to the local studio photographer and had them 'watch the birdie' so Daddy could carry about an image of the family while serving abroad. The picture-frame motif is seen (in conjunction with 'circus' lettering and a nice period radio set) in an advertisement for Sobell Radio of 1946; in a publicity handout for that marvellous film of the same year, *Brief Encounter;* in the cover of *Punch*'s summer number, 1948, and in advertisements for products as disparate as Jaguar motor cars and Yardley 'Bond Street' perfume.

Design for Guy Georget for Laboratories Geigy, France 1948

Wall lamp with white-lacquered brass mount held in a bronze hand; satin glass globe. Height 47cm (18½in.). Designed and made by Fontana Arte, Italy 1958

Hand motif: advertisement for the Portuguese National Secretariat of Information's Exhibition, Lisbon 1952

Motif from an advertisement for Ibeco waterproof packing paper. Anon., *Packaging and Display Encyclopedia*, 1948

Surrealism

A motif prolifically used between the war years and the late fifties was of disembodied hands. One can give innumerable examples, among them the jacket for the autobiography (1946) of the fashionable hairdresser (or as he preferred to say, 'hair sculptor') Antoine; the jacket of the *Contact* book 'Britain between East and West'; in boldly stylized form, on the cover of Walter Allen's *Black Country* (1948); in advertisements for ICI (1948), the National Health Service of Hungary (1948), *Arte Comercial,* Spain, (1948), Laboratoires Geigy, France (1948), Lewis Berger and Sons, Australia (1948), Container Corporation of America (1952), Radio Fridor (1952), and the Portuguese National Secretariat of Information's Exhibition, Lisbon (1952). Also in jacket designs for *Knitting Illustrated* (1949), The National Cash Register Company (1949), and *Three Ghosts,* illustrated by Laurence Scarfe (1949), an elegant pottery vase by Mitsusuke Tsuji of Japan (1955), and a wall-lamp designed and made by Fontana Arte, Italy (1958).

To some degree this was no doubt a manifestation of the Surrealist influence. Certainly that is the impression given by John Keir Cross's 'eighteen strange stories', *The Other Passenger* (1944), of which the illustrations by Bruce Angrave are the most elaborate example I know of the disembodied hand motif. One of Keir Cross's sinister stories is actually called 'Hands':

Advertisement for ICI by John R. Barker, 1948

Light and Colour

There is no need to put a hand into a glove to know of what it is made. For the eye can often distinguish one material from another by the way the light is reflected from its surface, each different texture producing its own visual effect. From this subtle interplay of light and surface arises the beauty of the many new materials now appearing in a multitude of shades—thanks to the use of dyes.

Cover by Edward Bawden for *Contact*, 1947

And the horror increased – she raised her hands to her flabby mouth as she saw him take from his pocket a thing she at first imperfectly recognized. Screaming now he waved it towards her. He held it in one hand and, with the trembling fingers of the other, felt at the bloody stump of it. He found what he wanted – the slimy end of the long tendon. Foam edged his lips as he held the beastly thing out at her and jerked the grisly cord. The mottled, clayey fingers of the hand grasped hideously at the air – like the claws of a chicken when the tendon is pulled.

Illustration by Bruce Angrave to 'Hands' in John Keir Cross' *The Other Passengers*, 1944

Illustration by Bruce Angrave to 'Miss Thing and the Surrealists' in John Keir Cross' *The Other Passenger*, 1944

46

47

Another of the stories, 'Miss Thing and the Surrealists', makes the connection between surrealism and disembodied hands more explicitly:

> We lived in those days in a constant turmoil. Artists we were most consciously – Surrealists moreover for the Movement was at its fashionable height then. . . . The handle of Kolensky's door was a Hand – a white and beautifully made wax Hand. It was held a little open and at the wrist there was a small circlet of lace that covered the join of it to the wood of the door. . . . The Hand then was the first of Miss Thing. The other Hand was inside the studio – but let me take all in order. . . . The truth was that Miss Thing (it was Howard's name for the personality she undoubtedly became in our minds) was Kolensky's studio. He lived almost literally *in* Miss Thing. . . . There were of course the Parts. Protruding inconsequentially from a wall there was a beautiful rounded Breast of coloured wax. The other Breast stood on a table. It had holes pierced in it symmetrically all round and flowers stuck out of these like the glass things people in the suburbs use. (Daffodil time showed the Breast at its best I think.) . . . The Navel was a little bell-push – you pressed it and an electric bell rang away in the basement for the desolate old woman who did Kolensky's charring. . . .
>
> And the other Hand? . . . When you were visiting Kolensky you went perhaps into the lavatory. At the end of the flush chain and like the one on the door half open to be grasped was the other Hand. Here again – to their embarrassment – the uninitiate had been known to turn away.

Certainly Surrealism had some part in popularizing the disembodied hand and indeed the disembodied anything else. But I feel that after the war the hand theme is more likely to represent the idea of remaking the world. Here there is a good parallel in primitive art, where the psychological bases of art can be seen in their raw, unaffected form. Mr William Fagg, Director of the Museum of Mankind, British Museum, London, in commenting on the Benin Oba's *ikegobo* or 'altar of the hand' (a superb bronze piece decorated with just such chopped-off hands as appear in European design in the forties and fifties) writes:

> The hand, in a ritual context, signifies a man's power to do things, i.e. his own ability to achieve success in material and practical things. Its worship is particularly characteristic of warriors. . . .[13]

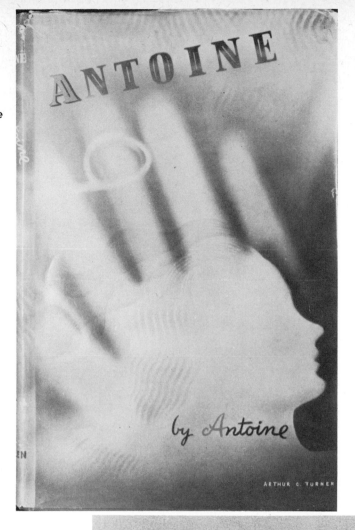

Jacket by Arthur
Turner for *Antoine*
by Antoine, 1946

Cover of Walter Allen's
The Black Country

The Post-war temper

The mood of Britain and Europe after the First World War had been one of relief, which was expressed in hectic celebration and a general frivolity in design. It took the Depression of 1929 to sober men down and to persuade designers to veer in the direction of hardness and simplicity.

After the Second World War, although casualties had been only a third of those of the First, there was little of this effervescence to be seen, though there was some: *Vogue* archly advised its whey-faced readers in 1947 'Be Bee-Stung in Two Shades of Rosy-Posy'. Far more than the Great War, the Second World War had hit civilians, had kept them at a constant pitch of tension, and thoroughly exhausted them. Britain and Europe were shabby and tired. The late Elizabeth Bowen expressed the mood of the time with a novelist's skill in the periodical *Contact* for 1946. She and her contemporaries, she said, were like 'goldfish in a bowl of exhausted water'.

> The world has been bad before – but did that, till lately, prevent the individual from conducting his life with a sort of secret assurance, a devout energy ? . . . What has become of the nerve of pleasure, the capacity for play : have these atrophied ?

She suggested that people would have difficulty in relaxing, and one phrase in the following passage suggests that those who had seen one ecstatically celebrated peace disrupted were not going to make fools of themselves by placing too much faith in another :

> We dread being thrown back on our own resources. Indeed, how many sneers at 'planning' arise from mistrust of what should be, intrinsically, its good effects ? Should catastrophe not again submerge us, we are due, in a reckoned number of years, each to be dealt out his or her accredited slab of leisure, leisure vested in safety. The energy-stimulus will be lacking ; the hypnotic rush for survival will have died down. We shall have no alibi. For hours of a day, not impossibly for days of a week, a benevolent state will require of us only that we should be ourselves. Liberty, and the pursuit of happiness . . . what were desiderata become perils.

It may be possible to detect in this the rancour against the Welfare State of a member of the upper-middle classes, resentful of the breaking-down of class barriers which had assured them of a comfortable life. One discerns also that characteristic Victorian trait of associating moral rectitude with pain (the Passion being a respectable precedent) – the educational idea that 'It doesn't matter what you teach the child, so long as he doesn't enjoy it', and the social idea that the Devil finds work for idle hands. 'Mechanically,' Miss Bowen continues, 'home life will proceed with increasing smoothness: no more drudgery, no more sacrificed persons. We shall be confronted, at every turn, by means to express and complete ourselves.' The hint was that only those traditionally trained to do so – the Bowens and their like – would be able to relax in an edifying way, even though the abolition of 'sacrificed persons' (e.g. domestic servants) would make it harder for them to do so, and might force them to wash dishes as well as write novels.

When idling is again an approved industry. When lawns sprout where brussels grew. When 'you've had it' becomes 'we have it, sir.' When once again there are those easy-cut 'Viyella' Sports Shirts that are cool when it's hot and warm when it's not. Why, it'll be peace again!

Advertisement for Viyella shirts, *Photo World*, April 1946

The classes not traditionally schooled in leisure did not share Miss Bowen's qualms. Though the mood might be lassitude rather than euphoria, the advertisers were quick to exploit it. In April 1946 Viyella Shirts invented the word 'lazyboning' – for 'when idling is again an approved industry. When lawns sprout where brussels grew. When ''you've had it'' becomes ''we have it, sir''. When once again there are those easy-cut ''Viyella'' Sports Shirts that are cool when it's hot and warm when it's not. Why, it'll be peace again!'

The nerve of pleasure was not dead. Designers, while they did not take flight into the wild fantasies and total frivolity of so many 1920s artists, wanted a bit of razzle – or Binge – after being forced for five years to keep to the official specifications of Austerity. There was to be no return to the self-righteous functionalism of the 1930s. The designer Geoffrey Boumphrey put the case for an injection of gaiety with sense and moderation (*Contact* no. 15, July 1949):

> I myself was never a functionalist in the sense that I wished all contemporary design to be limited to stark function, and expected thereby to see beauty achieved. But I did feel between the wars that we were suffering from an attack of what might be called aesthetic indigestion, consequent upon a surfeit of mixed and over-rich design diet, and I therefore advocated a purgative period during which we should subsist on little more than the bare essentials. . . . Today I find that my intellectual standpoint has changed little – but emotionally it is quite another story. After years of austerity and utility I feel a need for ornament, gaiety, and pattern.

The greatest difference between post-war design and that of the pre-war period, is that after the war France was no longer the dominant influence. In the Art Deco period, France set the style for most of the rest of Europe (one must except the triumphant Dutch Deco of the Tuschinski Cinema, Amsterdam). But now, after years of occupation, France was a spent force – not only culturally, but in a sense morally. In Britain particularly, where the feeling was that the last-ditch exhortations of Churchill would have been followed if the Germans had invaded, there was a general belief that, in spite of de Gaulle's courage and the activities of the Resistance, the French had submitted in a way which, if not actually craven, was far from heroic. How little the French now had to offer in cultural leadership is illustrated by the flaccid 1946 furnishing designs of René Gabriel, ranging from the limp, sagging lines of Jean Royère's bedroom scheme, to the sheer freakishness of E. Kohlmann's hideous dining-room suite, in which the feet of the table and sideboard are like miniature roll-top desks. It is symbolic that when the French government wanted a medal to commemorate the liberation, they commissioned one from Pierre Turin, the designer responsible for the pretty-pretty flower-garlanded medal of the 1925 exhibition. French design was stagnant.

E. Kohlmann, room design, Paris 1946

In default of a positive lead from Paris, an 'international' style, the British and Americans looked to their own traditional cultures for inspiration: The ornament, gaiety and pattern for which Geoffrey Boumphrey felt a need, they found in the bright, bold motifs of folk art. In England this meant in particular adopting designs from the circus, the fairground, gypsy caravans and painted narrow-boats (improperly called 'barges') of the English canals. Men who had been away from their own land for years, men who were sick of the Continent and its embroilments, rediscovered their own country with a kind of infatuation. My father is a good example: having spent the war sweltering in Aden, he cycled round the countryside making sketches, and in 1951 published his first book, *Old Surrey Watermills,* lovingly describing in word and ink illustrations (with wood-engraved jacket) that ancient folk craft. There was a renewed interest in writers such as W. H. Hudson, Richard Jefferies[1] and Edward Thomas, who wrote of English flora, fauna and folk; Gilbert White of Selborne; 'George Bourne' (George Sturt) of Farnham, who wrote *The Wheelwright's Shop,* and William Cobbett of the *Rural Rides,* another Farnham man. It was a heyday for the concocters of rambles, the highway-and-bywaymen such as Arthur Mee and S. P. B. Mais. Each weekend hundreds of wan Londoners took the train to the starting-point recommended by 'Fieldfare' of the *Evening News* and doggedly tramped round the route he had charted ('Note the ha-ha in front of Blackadder House. Turn left by the cherry tree in Parker's Yard.') For blitz-jaded Cockneys, it was the last great age of hop-picking holidays in the Weald of Kent, where they made money, got healthy and drunk, and helped fight the beer shortage; by the mid-sixties they were taking their vacations in Majorca and Torremolinos. Publishers, led by Batsford and Penguin, produced a spate of books on English crafts, traditions, wild flowers, inn-signs, butterflies and beetles. As early as 1943 the yearning for the essential England was expressed in E. L. Grant Watson's *Walking with Fancy,* illustrated by C. F. Tunnicliffe. As the epigraph to his book, Grant Watson had chosen some lines of Sir Henry Taylor's, ending:

> For thought is tired of wandering o'er the world
> And homeward fancy runs her bark ashore.

Vignette by C. F. Tunnicliffe for E. L. Grant Watson's
Walking with Fancy, 1943

Canal boats

John O'Connor, wood-engraved vignette for *Canals, Barges and People* Art and Technics, 1950

There was great interest among writers and artists in that quintessentially English bark, the canal narrow-boat, and in inland water travel generally. A significant number of books on canal craft was published between 1944 and 1960.[2] A caption in a book by the most prolific author on canal boats, L.T.C. Rolt, gives some idea of the folk mystique atached to canal craft: 'The rudder post of a Narrow Boat decorated with geometrical design, brightly coloured paint and white ropework. The entwined bands are called Turk's Heads, the vertical piece at the stern is a Swan's Neck, while the rudder post itself is known as a Ram's Head, thereby no doubt revealing an age-old link with the Long Ships of the Norsemen.' The almost masonic argot of the rivers gave people a cosy feeling of belonging. 'Sometimes,' Brian Waters confided in *Severn Tide* (1947), 'an elver tide, full of promise, has a disappointing ebb at Maismore if the flood-head sweeps the elver past the weir.'

A fine 'Barge on the Grand Union Canal' was illustrated by Noël Carrington and Clarke Hulton in *English Popular Art* (1945). Another good example appeared on the cover of *Photo World* for April 1946. An article inside by A. Christopherson, 'Water Gypsies' (a term invented by A. P. Herbert in the 1930s) carried the blurb: 'The traditions of the canal folk are dying. The trade of Britain's inland waterways must be kept alive.' It began:

'Barge On the Grand Union Canal' from *English Popular Art* by Noel Carrington and Clarke Hulton, 1945

Cover of *Photo World*, April 1946

You've got to be born to 'the Cut'. You've got to *know* barges. It's a family business, see? You land-lubbers seem to think it's a question of riding the horse along nice quiet tow-paths and seeing England the easy way. Swear like a bargee, you say. Gor strewth, mister, a bargee's got plenty to swear about, I c'n tell yer.

And Christopherson gave a good description of the artistic resources of the canal craft:

The 'boats', the long, narrow, canal barges with living-quarters in the stern and a rusty chimney poking to heaven, are a fantastic patchwork of gypsy art. 'Castles and Roses' are the traditional theme, and they are to be found on cabin walls, on doors and even on the gleaming buckets lashed to the cabin roof. Tillers and stanchions gleam with barber-pole designs. Hearts and flowery arabesques deck every available inch of superstructure. This is a sign of caste. The Brahmin among barges will look like a sign-painter's nightmare. The Untouchable will display a few half-hearted scrawls. The women relieve their thwarted domesticity by hanging the already cluttered cabins with old china plates, robust family and patriotic portraits, scintillating horse brasses and flouncy lace curtains. There is enough concentrated décor in one of them to furnish two normal-sized rooms and in the midst of this claustrophobic finery they live, sleep and raise their families.

During the war the Government took over all canals from private enterprise and recruited girl volunteer crews. One of the women volunteers was Susan Woolfitt, whose delightful book about her experiences, *Idle Women,* captures the authentic wartime blend of making-do and derring-do. Chapter I, 'How It All Started', begins:

> It was the end of the day; all the innumerable evacuees and visitors had gone to bed and I was sleepily tidying up downstairs before going up myself. Someone had left a paper on the table in the hall; it was folded back at a picture showing a girl, standing on top of a barge with a boat-hook in her hand, in a kind of 'Come to the Broads' attitude. I love boats, so it caught my eye. That was all. . . .
>
> The photograph was published at the instigation of the Ministry of War Transport, who were doing one of their periodic recruiting campaigns for the Women's Training Scheme. Women were being trained to work as canal boatwomen (or 'bargees' as most people mistakenly call them) in order to release men for the Armed Forces. This much I learned from the paper and instantly started to wonder if it was work that I could do.
>
> Both the children would be going off to boarding school in a week or so's time and I should then be free to do some real war work. . . .

She found herself working on narrow-boats about 70 feet (20 metres) long and seven feet (two metres) wide; they worked in pairs, one with a heavy-oil engine towing the other which was called a 'butty-boat'. There were three women to a crew. They would collect a cargo in Limehouse, empty it in Birmingham and pick up a cargo of coal in Coventry to empty in the London area. The boats travelled at five m.p.h. unloaded, and three to three and a half m.p.h. loaded. There were 152 locks between London and Birmingham. Mrs Woolfitt, who was to work in the children's term time only, was put to work after two training trips, and had a whale of a time. She, too, revelled in the narrow-boat jargon:

Quad Crown poster designed by John Piper for the Ealing Studios Film *Painted Boats*, 1945

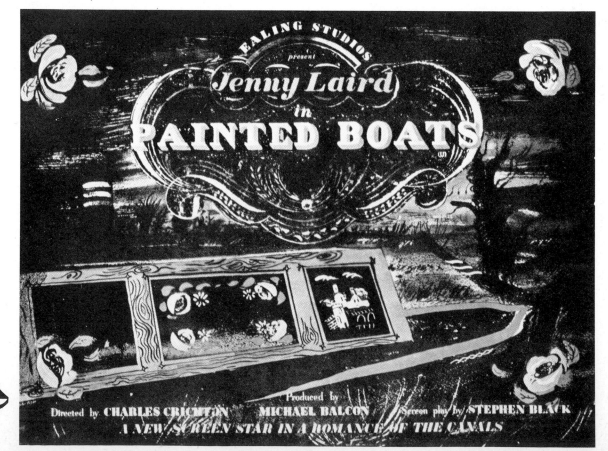

Every single part of a narrow-boat has its special name which in nearly every case is quite different from that used on sea-going or river craft. If you wanted to be particularly rude about an untidy narrow-boat, you would greet them as they went past with 'How d'you do, *sailor*!'

Like so many people involved in the war effort, Mrs Woolfitt suffered a feeling of anti-climax at the end of hostilities:

For some time after VJ Day I went on thinking that I should be able to go back . . . but by the end of the summer holidays I knew it was a vain hope. On every side I had news of the women packing up and going home. . . . There was nothing left but to go and collect my stuff from the store, which I did; an ultra-depressing business. . . . They laughed when I said I was 'a lady of leisure again' – as I meant them to do – but I felt more like crying.

For so many millions of people all over the world the war brought horror, torture, loss, that it seems almost wrong to have found anything good in what it brought to me; but it would be less than honest not to admit that it *did* bring me good.

All these things I have enjoyed and loved: the work of the boats, the pleasure of slowly learning to manage them, the shape and the colour and the noise of them; the homeliness of the cabins and the friendship of my fellow-workers; enormous appetites and the hundred per cent feeling of physical fitness, the tiredness and the heavenly rest at the end of the day; the colour of the cut through the seasons, the never-ending anticipation of what lay 'just round the corner' . . . the early mornings and the late evenings and the quiet black nights; the noise of the lock gates banging shut, the feel of the sun soaking into me as I lay full stretch on the balance beam, listening to the water boiling and racing below me . . . the complete stillness that suddenly fell when the panting engine was stopped at the end of the day.

Mrs Woolfitt's book is very engaging, and together with her book for children, *Escape to Adventure* (1948) about the Grand Union Canal (with excellent illustrations by Rosemary Hay, including a frontispiece of a girl leaping from the bank on to the roof of a boat) conveys better than any other book I know the pleasures of the canal life. At the same time, the characteristic 1940s note of class is there: the children are nicely packed off to their boarding school, leaving mummy free to help win the war; and there is this passage of almost charming naïveté:

There was a lot of talk before the war about the scandal of our slums. I never heard anyone mention the slums on the water—the bright paint of the boats and the golden summer fields through which they glide is so idyllic a picture with which to lull the conscience—picturesque is the word, or gipsy-like.

In 1947 responsibility for the canals was removed from the British Transport Commission and vested in a new Inland Waterways Authority. With holidays abroad out of the question for most people, holidays on English and Welsh canals gained in popularity. In 1945 John Piper designed a poster of the Ealing Studios film *Painted Boats* (director Charles Crichton, producer Michael Balcon; the principal star was Jenny Laird). In 1949 the first issue of the new *Image* magazine (edited by Robert Harling) published a wood-engraving of 'The Butty Girl' in an article on the wood engravings of John O'Connor. It was described as 'Engraving for a projected book on coastal and canal craft', and in fact this book was published in 1950. Wood-engraving, incidentally, was another craft being enthusiastically revived in the forties and fifties.[3] Winifred McKenzie's strong engraving, *House over the Canal, Bath,* was also executed in 1950.

Magazines took a continuing interest in canals and narrow-boats. *Everybody's* of 19 March 1949 blazoned its cover with the line 'Canals Crisis' and inside was an article by L. T. C. Rolt on the post-war difficulties of the boatmen under the newly constituted Docks and Inland Waterways Executive. The cover of *John Bull* of 28 August 1954 gave a less gloomy picture of canal life; the caption read:

> Every year, nearly five thousand canal pleasurecraft nose out miles of unspoilt countryside. And the number grows—a contrast to today's industrial neglect of our canal system. Michael Streat, of Braunston, Northants., has turned two old barges— Nelson and Nancy—into Britain's first inland floating hotel. One barge is a lounge, galley and dining-saloon; the other has eight sleeping cabins. K. J. Petts shows them at Stoke Bruern lock.

The issue of the same magazine for 12 October 1957 contained an optimistic article by Harry Hopkins, 'A Bustling Future for Our Canals'. In America, the equivalent of the narrow-boat, in folk-tradition terms, was the old Mississippi paddle-steamer, as shown on the covers of a Puffin book *Waterways of the World* (1946) and Frances Parkinson Keyes' novel of the same year, *The River Road*.

Wood engraving by John O'Connor from *Canals, Barges and People*, Art and Technics, 1950

Wood engraving by Winifred McKenzie, 'House over the canal, Bath' 1950

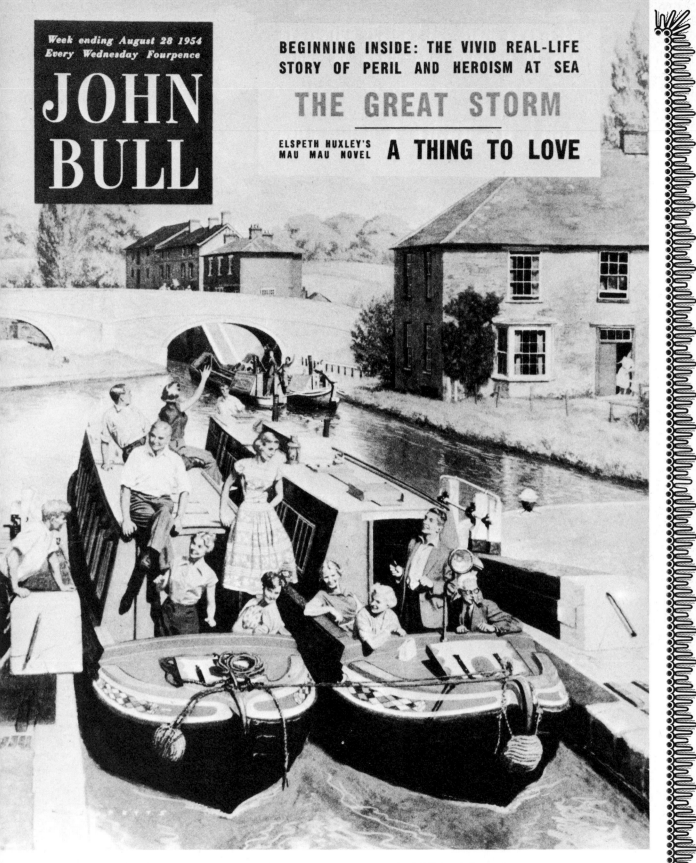

JOHN BULL

BEGINNING INSIDE: THE VIVID REAL-LIFE STORY OF PERIL AND HEROISM AT SEA

THE GREAT STORM

ELSPETH HUXLEY'S MAU MAU NOVEL **A THING TO LOVE**

Cover design by K. J. Petts for *John Bull*, 28 August 1954, showing Michael Streat's 'floating hotel' at Braunston, Northamptonshire

Gypsies, with their wooden caravans carved and painted in the harlequin colours of an ancient folk tradition, and with their Romany dialect, blood-mixing weddings and footloose-and-fancy-free way of life, had an equal appeal. This was not entirely new: it developed from the interest in gypsies (descending from George Borrow) shown by Augustus John, by the painter and wood-engraver Ethelbert White and his wife Betty, who often went on their travels in a gypsy caravan,[4] or from the idiotic idealization of gypsy life in Edward Teschemacher's *Romany Songs* of the early 1900s, including:

Where my caravan has rested,
Flowers I leave you on the grass,
All the flowers of love and memory,
You will find them when you pass.

You will understand their message,
Stoop to kiss them where they lie;
But if other lips have loved you,
Shed no tear—and pass them by.

Gypsies

'Gypsy Caravan' from *English Popular Art* by Noel Carrington and Clarke Hulton, 1945

(A similar idealization, though in better verse, is Robert Louis Stevenson's 'The Roadside Fire' which was set to music by Vaughan Williams in 1905, four years before 'Where My Caravan Has Rested' was given its lugubrious melody by Hermann Löhr.)

The great F. E. Smith, the first Lord Birkenhead, was fond of claiming gypsy blood[5] and his daughter, Lady Eleanor Smith, who became a passionate champion of gypsies and circus folk, wrote the plot of the 1946 film *Caravan*, starring Stewart Granger and Jean Kent, about an adventurer sent to deliver a valuable necklace in Spain, waylaid by enemies, and found and cared for by a gypsy girl. In a later film, *The Gypsy and the Gentleman* (1958), with Merlina Mercouri and Keith Michell, the villain tries to cheat his sister out of her inheritance to keep his gypsy lady friend in a proper manner. Carrington and Hulton illustrated a typical caravan in *English Popular Art* (1945). An article by Ross Gordon in *Photo World* of May 1946, entitled 'It's the Gypsy in Them', contained an amusing account of how the gypsies were affected by the war:

During the war, the Ministry of Labour was faced with conscripting of Gypsies for national service. How to trace them? They were not registered and had no set abode. When the authorities caught up with them they would protest they could neither read nor write – which is true of a large percentage – and then, having bluffed their way through the original interview, move on overnight. The trouble with all Gypsies is that they look alike. They found no difficulty in living without ration books. Tea they make from nettles. There is always meat in the hedge-rows if you know how to snare a rabbit, poach a pheasant or cook a hedge-hog in clay. Vegetables? Why queue at a Co-op when the ground is bursting with turnips and potatoes? And when you've been harvesting during the autumn it is a poor housewife who cannot fill the caravan with sufficient flour to make bread for the coming winter. Thus they lived on unmolested by the War.

Along came a Gypsy called E. A. Williams, the young, patriotic heir to his tribe's kingship. This Williams, a factory roof-spotter, protested to the Ministry that he wished to be in the Army. His request was refused. Eventually Williams came to London, saw the Ministry and threatened to desert his job unless put into the forces. Gypsy Williams ended by seeing Ernest Bevin and getting the job of putting his people into war work and national service.

Bevin gave Gypsy Williams a bicycle and a roving commission. On the bicycle he covered 370 miles a month. On the strength of his commission he visited isolated caravans and encampments, talked to the people in their own tongue, persuaded thousands of them to work for farmers as small family communities. Williams found one family who didn't even know there was a war on.

'Do you not see the papers?' Williams asked. They explained that they were unable to read. 'Have you not noticed anything unusual?' The head of the family said that they never went near the towns but that they *had* noticed a lot of flying machines and some loud noises. At the end of the conversation, four sons volunteered for the forces and subsequently went into the Commandos. . . . Yet another Williams conscript to the forces became a Spitfire pilot who shot down five Jerries although he was unable to read or write when enlisted in the RAF.

Walter Starkie's *Raggle-Taggle: Adventures with a Fiddle in Hungary and Roumania* (1949), gave the reaction of Continental gypsies to the recent war.[6] Nazi persecution brought to England and America (including the Walt Disney studios) refugees from the Continent with strong memories of European gypsy tradition.

The gypsy theme: Brahms double concerto in A minor, played by Heifetz, Feuerman and the Philadelphia Orchestra, USA late 1940s

BRAHMS. DOUBLE CONCERTO IN A MINOR FOR VIOLIN, CELLO AND ORCHESTRA
Played by Heifetz, Violin · Feuermann, Cello · Philadelphia Orchestra, Ormandy, Conductor
VICTOR RECORDS

CARAVAN

A GAINSBOROUGH PICTURE DISTRIBUTED BY

GFD

WILL BREAK BOX-OFFICE RECORDS
The Press Tells You Why :—

" With the names of Stewart Granger and Jean Kent on the canopy ' Caravan ' will soar to the same popular success as ' Madonna Of The Seven Moons ' . . . . . Millions of cinemagoers are hungry for such make-believe—plus Stewart Granger."—Ewart Hodgson, NEWS OF THE WORLD.

" Stewart Granger in a costume piece by Lady Eleanor Smith—is there any greater British box-office certainty ? . . . . . . Every audience will be greatly entertained by it." Moore Raymond, SUNDAY DISPATCH.

" . . . . . it will take and make enormous sums of money." Elspeth Grant, DAILY SKETCH.

" To all those who queued to see ' Madonna Of The Seven Moons " and ' The Wicked Lady,' the latest Gainsborough excursion will be the joy-ride of their lives."—Richard Winnington, NEWS CHRONICLE.

" . . . . . . the best and sturdiest possible contrivance for showing off the talent and charm of a new British film star, Stewart Granger."—Paul Holt, DAILY EXPRESS.

" A worthy successor to ' The Wicked Lady ' and ' Madonna Of The Seven Moons.' Stewart Granger, Anne Crawford and Jean Kent will charm their undoubtedly numerous admirers."—Joan Lester, REYNOLDS NEWS.

"A very satisfying entertainment of the romantic melodrama type . . . . . . Another highly successful raid on the realm of romance by Gainsborough Pictures."—Reg Whitley, DAILY MIRROR.

" A ' must ' for exhibitors . . . . they will have their hands full controlling the queues."—DAILY FILM RENTER.

" Sure-fire box-office."—THE CINEMA.

" Its commercial success is assured."—KINE WEEKLY.

STEWART GRANGER
JEAN KENT · ANNE CRAWFORD
DENNIS PRICE
with ROBERT HELPMANN

**RELEASE DATE
JUNE 3rd.**

GENERAL FILM DISTRIBUTORS LTD., 127-133 Wardour Street, London, W.I.

Hand-out advertising the Gainsborough film *Caravan*, 1946

Other countryside figures of folk tradition who seemed friendly and welcome were the water diviner and the scarecrow. Water-divining, a form of natural magic, had been revived in the war for practical reasons. Louis MacNeice's poem 'The Dowser' was written in September 1940 :

> And the hazel rod bent, dipping, contorting,
> Snake from sleep ; they were right
> Who remembered some old fellow
> (Dead long ago) who remembered the well.
>
> 'Dig', he said, 'dig',
> Holding the lantern, the rod bent double,
> And we dug respecting his knowledge,
> Not waiting for morning. . . .[7]

The scarecrow was a popular figure from Ray Bolger's portrayal of one in the film *The Wizard of Oz,* made in 1939 and repeatedly shown during the war – the MGM children's classic adapted from a story by Frank L. Baum of a Kansas farm girl catapulted over the rainbow into the Land of Oz. Another popular scarecrow appeared in the Wurzel Gummidge stories played on British radio children's hour in the forties, with his earthy

Jacket design by Victor Reinganum for *Straw in the Hair* compiled and edited by Denys Kilham Roberts

Cover of *Water Divining* by S. N. Pike 1945

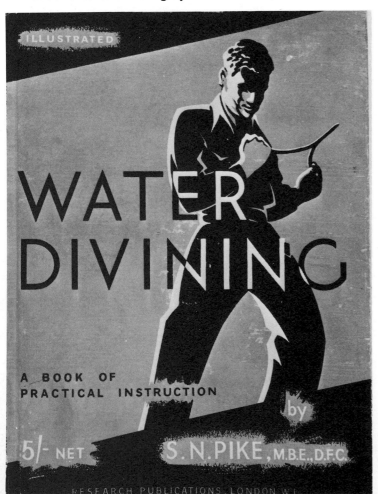

commonsense: 'Oo, ar; stands to reason'. A scarecrow figured on Victor Reinganum's jacket for *Straw in the Hair,* Denys Kilham Roberts's anthology of 'nonsensical and sur-realist verse'. Jean Picart le Doux designed a delightful scarecrow calendar for the Swiss printer C. J. Bucher in 1947. John R. Barker designed a similar scarecrow composition for Imperial Chemical Industries in 1949. Walter de la Mare, who had published one poem called 'The Scarecrow' in his First World War collection, *The Listeners* (1914), now pub-blished another in his 1945 collection, *The Burning Glass.* It is admittedly a sadder and wiser scarecrow than the 1914 one. The 1914 one confided that when spring came, 'Some rapture in my rags awakes'; the 1945 one cuts a sorry figure:

> In the abandoned orchard – on a pole,
> The rain-soaked trappings of that scarecrow have
> Usurped the semblance of a man – poor soul –
> Haled from a restless grave . . .[8]

But the scarecrow from the pop-gun game 'Crow Shoot', bought at Marks and Spencer's in 1948, is a friendly creature who evidently holds no terrors for the crows.

The strong interest in folk art and traditions affected many books and magazine articles at the time: directly, in books such as Margaret Lambert's and Enid Marx's *English Popular and Traditional Art* (1946), Noel Carrington's *Life in an English Village,* illustrated by Edward Bawden (1949), *English Popular Art* by Carrington and Hulton (1945), and Erwin O. Christensen's *Popular Art in the United States* (1948); indirectly, in books such as *The Country Heart* (1949) by H. E. Bates, with delicate Palmerish illustrations by John

'Crow Shoot': children's pop-gun game, bought at Marks and Spencer's, 1948

Jacket design by John Piper for Geoffrey Grigson's *An English Farmhouse*, 1948

Illustration from *Music Time* by Prudence Hemelryk and Sheila Jackson, 1947

Minton; John Hampson's *The English at Table* (1944) – one of an enormous series of 'Britain in Pictures' published by Collins; S. R. Badmin's *Village and Town* (1942); or Geoffrey Grigson's *An English Farmhouse* with John Piper jacket, of which the publisher's blurb said:

> In this highly individual book an artist, a descriptive writer and a colour photographer together look closely at one small corner of England. From the stones and thatch of its walls and roofs, the elm of its timbers, the detail of its site and surroundings emerges a lively picture of an English farmhouse and the physical and social changes through which it has lived.

Music Time (1950), a book of easy piano tunes for children by Prudence Hemelryk, with lithographs by Sheila Jackson, was a virtual compendium of English folk institutions – the punch-and-judy show, hobby-horse, jack-in-a-box, tin soldiers, witches, sailors and mermaids ('This is a sad little tune which the mermaids chant'), jesters, Noah's ark, hunting, gold procession coach, barrel organ, Guy Fawkes, snowman and maypole. Reginald Haggar's book, *English Pottery Figures, 1660–1860*, appeared in 1947. Haggar was the first ceramic historian to research thoroughly into such primitive Staffordshire potters as Obadiah Sherratt, whose earthenware 'Bull-baiting' group – as Olde English an object as can be conceived – Haggar illustrated in an ink drawing in *Apollo* annual, 1948. Bernard

Drawing by Reginald Haggar of an earthenware group of 'Bull-Baiting' attributed to the Staffordshire potter Obadiah Sherratt c. 1778-1850, *Apollo* annual 1948

Rackham's *Animals in Staffordshire Pottery* appeared in 1953. Pottery itself responded to the folk influence: the three copper-lustre jugs designed by S. C. Talbot and made by A. E. Gray and Co. in 1949 are hardly distinguishable from those of the nineteenth century (the kind of wares from which Piper adapted his central motif on the cover of *An English Farmhouse*); while in the Cincinnatti Museum can be seen a hand-thrown earthenware fruit dish by Edwin and Mary Scheier with decoration, incised through black glaze, based on *Johnny Appleseed,* an American folk legend. The cover of *John Bull* magazine of 27 August 1955 shows all that Englishmen had looked forward to returning to after the war. The caption inside read:

Pastiche of English early nineteenth-century pottery: two lustre-ware jugs designed by S. C. Talbot and made by A. E. Gray and Co. 1949

Sooner or later, almost everyone has a baptism in country lore, and usually haymaking is the ceremony. It's a trap that the country springs on even the most urbane of visitors to teach them how busy life is on the sleepy-looking land. But the effort is its own rich reward, and it's only in the long shadow of a day's work that cheese sandwiches and cold tea taste like a harvest feast. Ronald Lampitt's haymaking scene is set at Snowhill, his favourite among the quiet Cotswold villages. As an artist, his only regret is the square tidiness of modern hay bales compared with the soft shape of a traditional rick which was once the very symbol of the countryside.

Cover design by Donald Lampitt for *John Bull* 27 August 1955 showing harvesting at the Cotswold Village of Snowshill

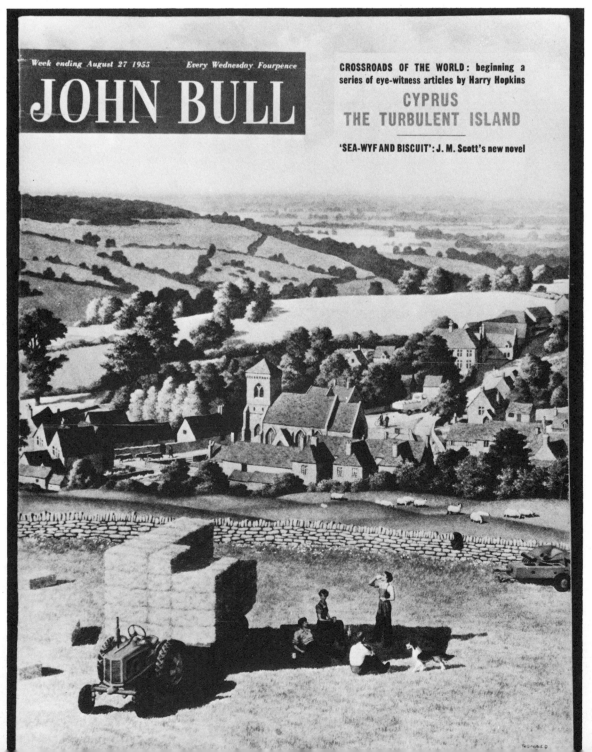

Week ending August 27 1955   Every Wednesday Fourpence

JOHN BULL

CROSSROADS OF THE WORLD: beginning a
series of eye-witness articles by Harry Hopkins

CYPRUS
THE TURBULENT ISLAND

'SEA-WYF AND BISCUIT': J. M. Scott's new novel

Circus and fairground

Jacket design for *Pamela* by Florence Gunby Hadath (n.d.). The blurb is a classic: 'Pamela is rather a unique character of a schoolgirl but this in no way detracts from her charm and lovableness ... Her closest friend, the faithful Martha Tydd, is the sort of friend that most girls would love to have: the resourceful Alice Winkerley and the dim-witted loutish Jane Clumberclutch go toward making this a brilliant funny book without lessening its charm.'

By far the most popular transmitter of folk art tradition was the circus in both England and America. As an index of public interest, over thirty books on the circus are recorded by *The English Catalogue of Books* for the years 1942-59.[9]

That list includes only books with the word 'Circus' in the title. It does not include John Guthrie's *Merry-Go-Round* (1950), Neil Paterson's *Man on the Tight Rope* (1953), or the new and revised edition of Noel Streatfeild's *The Circus is Coming* – with their spirited jackets. It also omits the most splendid book devoted to the circus in our period, Fernand Léger's *Le Cirque* (1950), a work in the same sumptuous tradition as Rouault's pre-war book of the same title. Enid Blyton, too, the children's writer most widely read in post-war Britain, brought the circus theme into many of her books. Circuses gave an unending supply of lovable animals and shady gypsy-like characters for the Famous Five and the Secret Seven to encounter; and even in her girls' school stories about 'Malory Towers' there is a girl from a circus background, Carlotta, whose manners, of course, are not quite what Malory Towers is used to. Neither does the list include books on the fairground; I remember what an impression was made on me in my own childhood by Patricia Lynch's fine and almost mystical book, *Strangers at the Fair* (1947). *The Twenty-one Balloons* (1949), written and illustrated with immense skill and invention by William Pène du Bois, showed armchairs and sofas that whizzed round the drawing room like dodgems, their tram-like aerials sparking shooting stars from the gridded ceiling.

Circus and fair figured prominently in the cinema too. Walt Disney's *Dumbo* (1941) was the story of a circus elephant who discovers he can fly; in researching the film, Disney's artists spent time sketching at the Cole Brothers' Circus for the circus parade and clown scenes. Columbia's *Tars and Spars*, billed as 'the top musical of 1946', and starring Alfred Drake, Janet Blair, and Marc Platt, had 'Love is a merry-go-round' as its main theme song. Although *Brighton Rock* had been written just before the war, the film made in 1947, with Richard Attenborough as Pinkie (produced and directed by the Boulting Brothers) made much of Kibber's meeting Ida in a funfair. Another film which made striking use of circus and fairground props was Paramount's *Variety Girl* (1947), which included a giant carousel. Moving into the 1950s, there are *One Good Turn*, the film in which Norman Wisdom, as janitor of an orphanage, tries to win money at the fair to buy the pedal-car one of the boys longs for (the camera follows him past hoop-la, shooting booth and coconut shy, with the tenacity of a dedicated private eye); the Hungarian film *Merry-go-round* (1955), directed by Zoltán Fábri, in which the lovers, Mari Törőcsik and Imre Sós, meet on the carousel of the title; *La Ronde*; and *Strangers on a Train*, Hitchcock's film which ends on a merry-go-round careering madly out of control.

Publicity handout for the Columbia film *Tars and Spars* 1946

Illustration from *Men Only*, showing Heather Pugh, of Cole Brothers Circus, leaping from a trampoline over a parked Chevrolet

The fascination the subject held is best illustrated in magazines of the time. The December 1946 issue of *Photo World* had as its cover a delightful colour photograph of a clown and a dancer. Inside was an article on clowns, including the Cairoli Brothers (in fact father and son) who were in London for the Christmas season. ('During the war the younger Cairoli worked hard in a war factory all day and rushed off at night to delight Palladium audiences with his act.') *Leader* Magazine of 27 May 1950 showed on its cover a Romany girl painting a carousel horse. *John Bull* ran a whole series of circus and fairground covers: dodgems (5 August 1950); roundabouts (12 May 1951); elephants (21 July 1951); Big Dipper (4 August 1951); clown with stilt legs (10 April 1954). A short-lived magazine founded in 1950 was actually called *Circus*. 'Victoria' MSIA, the talented silhouette caricaturist, designed circus cartouches for *The Sketch*, published by Constable. A

Cover design for *John Bull*, 5 August 1950, showing a dodgem rink

Advertisement designed by Raymond Tooby for Winsor & Newton, *Image*, 1950s

'Circus girl', heavy centre 30 cm (12 in.) vase, deeply engraved, designed by Deane Meanley, and executed by Ernest Rowley for Stevens and Williams, 1948

drawing in *Contact*, 1947, represented the BBC as a circus act.

Fascination with the circus could go very deep. In February 1946 *Photo World* published a profile of the colour-photographer John Hinde, by Humphrey Knight. It began:

> If you asked John Hinde what he thought about the future of colour photography, he would tell you: 'I'm not a photographer now, I'm the manager of a circus.' You might think that no kind of answer, but you would misjudge him. He will tell you about the colour pictures of tomorrow, but he will want you to understand that he is managing the circus first and taking pictures last.

The article described how Hinde had spent the war, in collaboration with Stephen Spender, producing a book on the British civilian at war. It continued:

> The recent success of *Citizens in War – and After* encouraged him to embark on another book. His publishers suggested the life of the circus as good pictorial subject. Lady Eleanor Smith wrote the book which was finished just before her death. When the idea of the circus was suggested, Hinde knew 'less than nothing' about the tenting circus. He joined up with a travelling circus touring Scotland. They gave him a small trailer (originally used by a chimpanzee) into which he stored all his equipment. This left very little room, about three feet, where he could put down his sleeping bag.

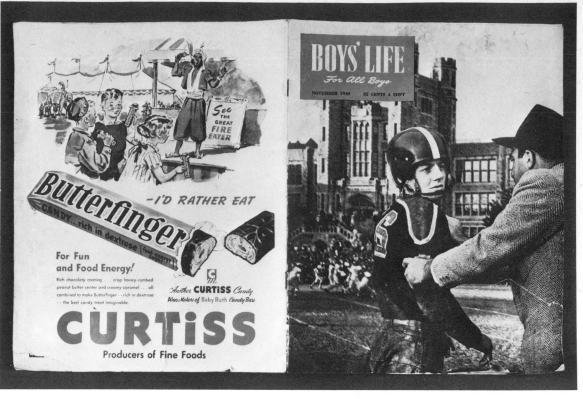

Cover of *Boys' Life*, USA November 1949

Pottery plate marked: '"Circus" by Beswick, England, Underglaze colours'. Late 1940s or early 1950s

Circus design on skirt. English, *c.* 1950

He found the life exciting enough, for a few days later one of the lions escaped. Everyone turned out to track down the lion, including the local Home Guard. They found him eventually under a hedge in the corner of a field. Employing tactics originally intended for more bitter enemies, the Home Guard encircled the King of Beasts with pikes and renovated Lee Enfields.

But the trainer arrived in time to avert a tragedy. The astonished J.H. watched him walk up to the lion, talk to it, and entice it into the waiting van. It was the talk of the village for weeks afterwards. Two days later the circus had forgotten it. Hinde soon learned that for them it was not unusual.

Hinde 'went on the road' and soon the varied and romantic life absorbed him. He grew to know the circus people, to like and respect them. He became entirely enthralled with the life. To-day he is leaving home to manage a circus. He is making it his job. The pictures for his new book are approaching completion. He is getting the life of a tenting circus into his portraits. But, if you ask John Hinde what he does, he will still tell you that he manages a circus and likes it.

In canvas painting and in drawing, Laura Knight remained the most prolific depictor of circus and fairground scenes, as she had been in the 1930s; but these subjects were now general favourites with artists. In the United States, the artist best known for his circus and carnival scenes was Reginald Marsh, who was born in Paris in 1898, came to America in 1900 and died in New York in 1954. The Metropolitan Museum of Art, New York, possesses a particularly spirited drawing by him, *Girl on Merry-Go-Round* in pen, ink and wash (dated 1948). Clowns were a favourite subject of Bernard Buffet in France, another great circus country.

The cover designs by John Verney for the children's magazine *The Young Elizabethan,* founded in England just before the Coronation, were often of circuses and fairs. William Roberts designed a splendid two-panel poster in 1951; one side showed swing-boats in careering motion, while the other side, words only, read:

The English Fairground has a tradition as old as London, and though new attractions and new thrills may be devised they will never supplant the roundabouts with their stiffly prancing steeds, the gaily painted swings, the coconut shies and the well-baited hoop-la stall. Nor will the romping blare of the organ down the street ever lose its compelling invitation.

Cecil Beaton designed for his cottage in Wiltshire a bed in the form of a carousel, complete with barley-sugar pillars: 'The only disappointment,' wrote a visitor ,'was that it did not revolve to barrel-organ music.'

Eric Brown and Barbara Jones (perhaps the leading spirit in British folk revivalism and herself an artist) contributed adjacent essays to *The Architectural Review* (February 1945) under the title 'Roundabouts; Demountable Baroque'. These articles go a long way towards explaining why the interest in circus and fairground was so great. Brown argued that the fairground had retained its exuberance because it was a working-class institution, free from interference by the genteel bourgeoisie. Could one, he asked, imagine a fairground designed by an architect from the London suburbs? He added:

The essential quality of unashamed heartiness remains, and the flabby hand of the gentlemanly designer has not yet been loosed in the field of fairground design. May that same quality which gives us the writing on the coster's barrow, on the cut-price store labels, and on the windows of the cheap 'Dining Rooms', continue in the decorating of the fair machines and may the slick American industrial designer be restricted to static streamlining and the architectural re-styler to his pale blue and gilt church furnishings.

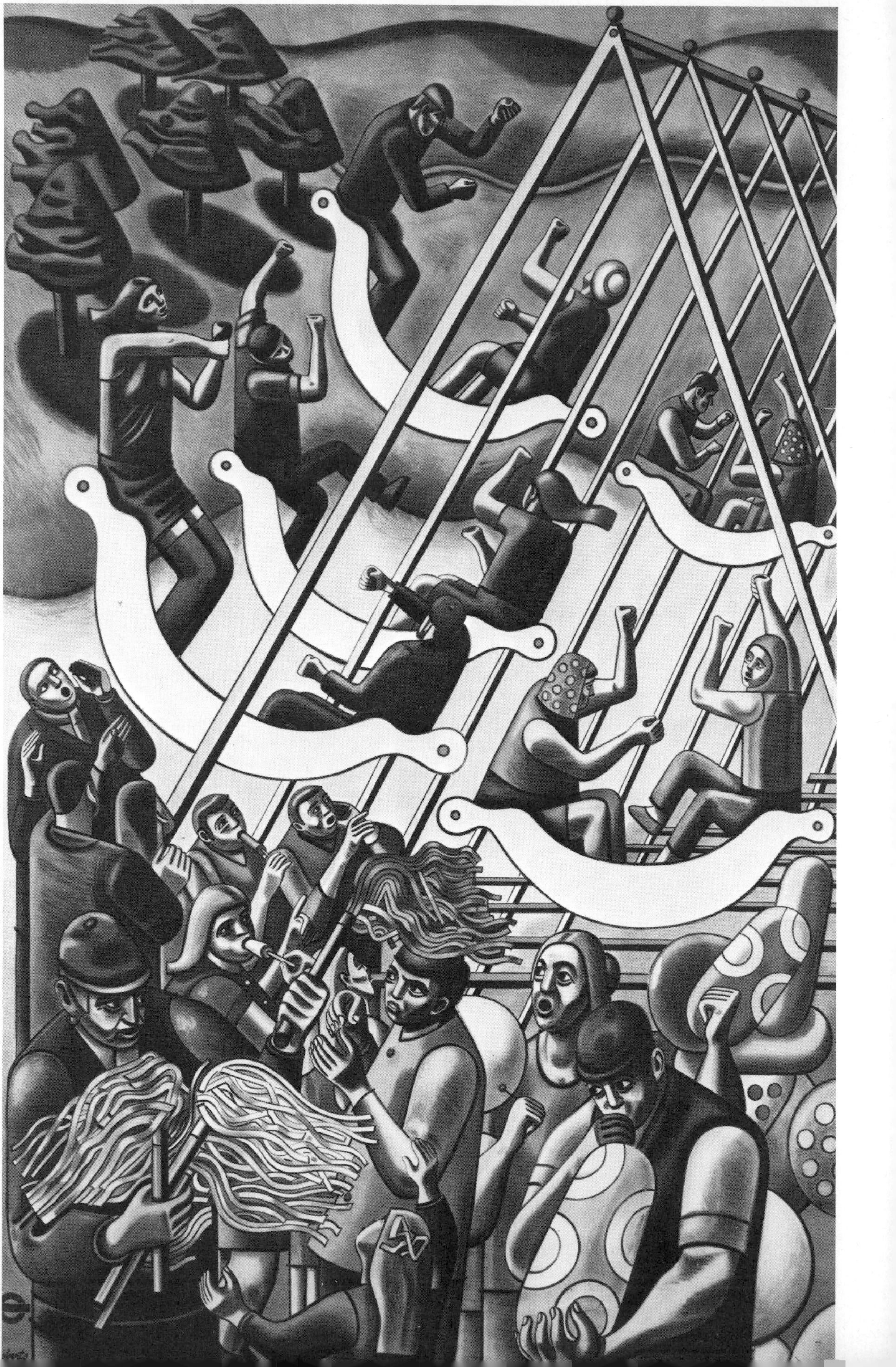

SHE WILL EXPECT THE BEST!

GIVE HER A *Vactric*

THE FINEST 'MAID'

It may be her knees or it may be her nylons—but you won't catch *her* bending!

Her line is dusting Dresdens—not brushing carpets or polishing floors. For such low level labour she's been used to the finest electrical appliances that money can buy, so she will expect *you* too to provide a Vactric vacuum cleaner and 3-brush floor polisher.

Ask your electrical dealer to demonstrate these labour saving devices that make molehills out of mountains of housework.

In next to no time the Vactric electric floor polisher puts a higher gloss on parquet, board, linoleum and tiled floors than hours of hand polishing can achieve

£18 18 0. Tax £7 1 9 extra.

Model R.45 vacuum cleaner incorporates a simple brush height adjustment for varying thickness of pile, and a special device which brings the handle to floor level for cleaning under low furniture.

£12 12 0. Tax £4 14 6 extra.

VACTRIC LTD., 149 REGENT STREET, LONDON, W.1.

London Fairs': poster by William Roberts, 951. (A text sheet was pasted up together ith this pictorial one)

Two British attitudes which obtained through the late forties and well into the fifties underlie this passage. First, the glorification of working-class culture. Many intelligent men of all classes were done with the Tory *ancien régime*. There was a score to settle with the politicians and establishment who had appeased Hitler before the war; and there was a score to settle with the same Old Guard who had seen to it that the men who had become officers and the men who were consigned to the ranks in the war were at the outset as rigidly stratified by social classes as in the First World War. The new educated working and lower-middle classes, who had smarted under the humiliation of Munich and chafed under the command of limp public-school officers who were often (though not of course always) less intelligent and resourceful than themselves, had the first chance to make their feelings known in the General Election of 1945 which produced, in spite of the overwhelming personal popularity of Churchill, a resounding victory for Labour. The forties and fifties were the last age of extreme class-consciousness in Britain; though to speak of the 'classless society' of the 1960s and onwards is to overstate the case.

In the forties an advertisement for Icilma Shampoo could (November 1946) show the head of an elegant woman, captioned: 'Softly curved chin – patrician nose . . . but she can't be beautiful without beautiful hair.' What copywriter today would attempt to sell his product by associating it with the word 'patrician'? Aged retainers were still in evidence in advertisements, too, such as 'Old Hethers', the ingratiating sidewhiskered butler who recommended Robinson's Barley Water – 'If you'll forgive me saying so' – right up to the late fifties. The officer-type in the Rose's Lime Juice advertisement from *Lilliput* may be painting his own greenhouse, but never fear, the butler, Hawkins, is bringing him out a tray of Rose's lime juice. The art editor of *Lilliput* in July 1941 still presumably thought the joke would be fairly universally appreciated when an 'Anton' cartoon showed a butler turning from the telephone to his master and saying: 'I asked the gentleman's secretary whether you were expected to wear a white or black tie, my lord – and she says it depends on whether you intend to wear "tails" or a dinner jacket.' If you couldn't have a butler, you could at least run to a maid or charwoman; so, at least, 'Vactric' vacuum cleaners hinted: 'She will *expect* the best!' However, the redoubtable expression of truculence on the face of the maid in question contrasts significantly with the servile deference an employer might have expected before the war. An advertisement for the 12-cylinder Lagonda

Wage 1948   Salary 1948   Capital 1948

She goes to work in Jaeger's neat
tailored suit in fine wool, modelled
with a flaring skirt on the newest
lines. It costs about six pounds

Company secretary is elegant and
workmanlike in Dorville's ceiling
price suit, about twenty pounds.
Accessories change for the evening

Digby Morton's beautiful suit re-
lies on exquisite material, pre-
cision tailoring, careful detail;
is only made to measure; expensive

Fashion page from *Contact*, 1948, showing a wage girl, a salaried girl, and a capital
girl. All look fairly well-heeled

1940 drophead coupé set it in front of the estate wall of a stately home; and though billed
as 'the first completely modern high quality car available to the public,' the car was a
supremely pre-war creation, with nothing of the forties about it – the kind of vehicle in
which 'The Saint', that pre-war hero, might have raced to a new adventure with a devil-
may-care look in his eyes.

Class was an important issue, which preoccupied the more serious publications. It was
significant that the tenth *Contact* book (1948), which faced 'the issue of ''Class'' in Britain
and abroad', was entitled 'Other People's Lives', indicating a privileged élite surveying
the *hoi polloi* with disdainful objectivity. Even so, the leading article, by Dr Colin Coote,
was headed 'The Barriers Fall'. Against Dr Coote's picture of improved education for all,
an expanding popular press, the rise of paperback books, and increased taxes on wealth,
could be set Philip Toynbee's essay, 'The Burden of Background'; an anonymous article
on 'The English Upper Class, 1948'; three pictures which compared the clothes of the
'wage' girl, the 'salary' girl and the 'capital' lady of 1948; and a cover which showed a
miner hacking away under the ground on which a carefree girl is sunbathing – anticipat-
ing by almost twenty years *Private Eye*'s satire on Sir Alec Douglas-Home's remark 'I have
lived among miners', which represented him striding across a grouse moor while a miner

burrowed beneath. No book today could seriously have the title which Kay Smallshaw, former Editor of *Good Housekeeping,* chose for a book published by John Lehmann in 1949: *How to Run Your Home Without Help.*

In *Les Voix de Silence* (1947) André Malraux wrote: 'There is no longer any folk art; because there is no longer any folk.' Certainly genuine peasants were hard to find, but in England, intellectuals desperately hunting for cultural roots discovered the industrial folk, almost as isolated from the wellsprings of fashion as a nineteenth-century rural peasant. The moony way in which it was possible to write of this urban folk tradition is illustrated in another *Contact* article, 'Ragamuffin Rag' by Mark Benney:

> The street games of London were among the prettiest of the by-products of urban industrialism. With their intricate playways and legend-haunted songs they were probably the only genuine products of a native proletarian culture. Thirty years ago, if a child of the middle classes had found himself in a Lambeth or Stepney back street on a May evening, he would have found the grey air flowering with play-chants he had never heard before, the grey pavements scrawled with play-symbols he had never seen, and a hundred grey little urchins treading play-measures as remote from his experience as any savage island dance.

It was in the forties that Peter and Iona Opie began their researches into playchants and nursery rhymes. Books appeared on the old broadsheet songs and accounts of Victorian executions, such as those printed by the Catnatch Press. The first performance of a ballet with a working-class setting, *Miracle in the Gorbals*, was given by the Sadler's Wells Ballet at the Princes Theatre, London, on 26 October 1944. The music was by Arthur Bliss, the ballet by Michael Benthall, the choreography by Robert Helpmann, and the décor by Edward Burra. America's slum-ballet came in the fifties with *West Side Story*. In Paris, peasant culture penetrated even the final citadel of aristocratic frivolity, *haute couture.* Lesley Blanch wrote in December 1948 of:

> Pierre Balmain, one of the most approachable [designers] who looks what he is, of tough Savoie stock, and who rolls around his showroom controlling every aspect of the business. . . . Balmain retains his Savoie ways in the Avenue François I, and, as a priest is usually brought to bless the pasturage, so he usually gets a priest friend to come along and bless the various new ventures – a hat salon, perhaps, or a new atelier.
>
> 'Bonjour, mon père,' say the mannequins, as the reverend father is sighted along the elaborate showroom, and nobody finds it the least bit incongruous.

The other British Austerity/Binge attitude implicit in the passage from Eric Brown's *Architectural Review* article is the strong anti-American feeling: 'may the slick American industrial designer be restricted to static streamlining. . . .' There were several causes of general anti-American feeling in Britain, some of them quite irrational. There was the sour feeling that America had entered the war late, and only after the direct assault on Pearl Harbor: a feeling which the American 'How we won the War' movies after the war did little to dissipate. There were unforgiving husbands whose wives had taken up with American servicemen billeted in England; there were even unforgiving wives who resented certain Americans' attempts to make them unfaithful – for this was the Unpermissive Society. The complaint: 'They're over-dressed, over-sexed, and over here' was a popular joke. Above all, there was the indecent richness of America: the food parcels sent with the kindest intention but grudgingly received by people who hated 'accepting charity'; the larger-than-life tourists with technicolor space-age cars whose silver-finned tails blocked the pavement when parked at right-angles; the steady flow into Britain of American pop culture – first chewing gum and bubble gum, later horror comics, rock 'n' roll, Elvis the Pelvis, and jukeboxes. The schoolteachers who disgustedly made their pupils spit out bubble gum, and who con-

77

American car of the 1950s

fiscated their American comics, called the invading culture 'brash', 'trash' and (as Eric Brown does in the passage quoted) 'slick'. Anti-American feeling reached its height in the late fifties, when the huge brazen American Embassy was put up among the quiet Georgian and Victorian mansions of Grosvenor Square. Not until the sixties, when British Beatle music and mini-skirts invaded America, did this feeling lessen. Not until the devaluation of the dollar in the seventies was it finally put to rest; and a British journalist, Jon Akass of *The Sun,* took that occasion to give what seems to me the best description of what the British had felt in the fifties:

> What I am going to do, by way of celebrating the most significant event in the financial history of the free world, is gloat.
>
> I am not all that damned old, I tell myself, but I do remember a time when all Americans seemed to be unbelievably wealthy and the dollar was downright magical.
>
> I was a give-us-some-gum-chum kid. I mislaid my youth in that austere post-war period when trousers were rationed. My adolescence had a pinched and utility look.
>
> At that time, it was not merely that the Americans seemed to enjoy an abundance of the things we cherished, like gaberdine, they were also physically larger. It was an impressionable time of my life and it gave me a severe turn, later, to be accosted in New York streets by American beggars.
>
> I was also surprised to find that Americans are not, striking an average, any bigger than we are. And that American cops are all incredibly fat.
>
> These discoveries, though, came too late to save my youth which had been dissipated in impotent envy.
>
> We pretended, we even convinced ourselves, that American cars were vulgar and flashy but what we lusted after, in our fantasies, was a car more vulgar and flashy still.
>
> They were never short of eggs. Their shoes had thick soles. Their jackets had wide lapels. They were able to supply nylons. Worst of all, they were all infuriatingly generous.
>
> You might be asking, here, what all this churlish rambling has to do with the most significant event in the free world's financial history. . . . The dollar has now been devalued, diminished. . . . And we Europeans, of a certain age, can now finally forgive her for once being wealthy when we were poor and so generous that it hurt.[10]

In America there was also a revival of interest in circuses – was this not the land of Barnum and Bailey? – and in other forms of folk art. In 1948 Erwin O. Christensen's book *Popular Art in the United States* was published. It dealt with Pennsylvania chests; the crafts of the Shakers; figureheads on whaling vessels; cider and pickle jars; and patchwork and appliqué quilts worked with names such as Kentucky Snowball, Rattlesnake Trail, Hen Scratch, Missouri Trouble, Indian Hatchet and World Without End. The Americans, like the English, were rediscovering their native inheritance, including the arts of the circus. Christensen wrote:

> When the straight bows of steamships gradually drove the figureheads from the high seas, the men who had made them turned to other carving, often to circus wagons and shop figures. The circus is a thoroughly American institution. Perhaps it was the lack of diversion in small rural communities, the need for variation and willingness to meet pleasure whole-heartedly, that gave the circus its opportunity . . . the picturesque publicity and exaggeration, the bluster and humbug that seemed to go with a circus was (sic) in keeping with the rough-and-tumble of an expanding country. Something of this spirit we feel in the gaudy decorations of the wagons.

One of Christensen's illustrations was of a panel from the circus bandwagon 'The United States', once owned by the Ringling Brothers' Circus. In the caption to this, he writes:

> To American boys and girls the country over, the circus was the apotheosis of all that was grand and splendid . . . . The decoration of the wagons, like this one with symbols of the United States lavishly gilded and carved with scroll-work, flags and figures, must have seemed supreme magnificence to those whose lives were spent in drab little towns.

Again, he illustrates a circus figure – a muse with a scroll:

> The muses of mythology may seem incongruous symbols for the circus, and yet they are well established in the world of popular amusement having come in through the theatre. Even the noisy steam organ of the circus was called a 'calliope', after the muse of epic poetry.

The figure in question was designed by the Sebastian Wagon Company for a Barnum and Bailey circus wagon. The carving was attributed to Samuel Robb, a well-known New York City carver.

As an example of the penetration of circus themes into American popular art of our period, I illustrate a page from the science fiction periodical *Fantastic Story Magazine* (1953). The illustration, which shows a lugubrious clown doffing his hat in the midst of nude houris, is captioned: 'Nobody could figure out how the clown got into the act – or what he was.' Looking at the picture, it seems fair comment.

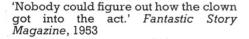

'Nobody could figure out how the clown got into the act.' *Fantastic Story Magazine*, 1953

The Oyster principle

In my two books on Art Deco, I was at pains to isolate the recurring motifs of the style – sun-ray, fountain, Aztec temple, racing dogs and so on – and to attempt explanations of why they became popular. Austerity/Binge also had its distinctive motifs, and some explanation has already been offered for the recurrence of circus and fairground themes. But there is another group of motifs, some of them equally often repeated, which owe their popularity to the post-war need to de-fang and make friendly the threatening symbols of war. If such a word existed, one might call this process 'amicization'. More picturesquely, one can compare it to the way in which an oyster converts a piece of grit into a pearl.

The most common of these motifs is the mermaid, and I do not think it far-fetched to suggest that this was a lyrical symbol for the seas' being free again of submarine and torpedo. Syrens instead of sirens, as it were.[11] Similarly, the recurring winged-horse or Pegasus motif of the later forties symbolized the new freedom of the air from menace. By the same process parachutes were visually converted into colourful balloons (besides being physically cut into lengths of silk for austerity clothing[12]). Heraldic decoration also became popular, as a way of making friendly the martial badges of wartime.

The Mermaid motif

The frequency of the mermaid motif in forties and early fifties decorative art is extraordinary. I have talked to more than one artist who was an art student at the time; they recall, with surprised recognition, that mermaids, like clowns and other circus themes, were among their design repertoire then. We see the motif here in the exuberant etched design of a forties pub mirror; on curtain fabric; on skirt material; on a cheap brooch; on plastic dishes and plates; and on a delightful piece of silver by Leslie Durbin MVO, a silversmith who was partly responsible for decorating the sword and scabbard presented by Britain to Russia in recognition of the heroic defence of Stalingrad. The finest interpretation is a glazed terracotta figure (page 40) bought in 1971 by the New York dealer Lewis V. Winter in the junk market at Englishtown, New Jersey. It is probably a French model of the late forties; certainly it could belong to no time before 1940, and to no time after 1960.

Gulliver

Goes Aboard The

Ocean Reaper

Cartouche by 'Victoria', *Lilliput*, January 1949

Public-house mirror with mermaid design, late 1940s

Detail from a skirt with mermaid motif

Moulded plastic dishes, olive-green, with mermaid motifs

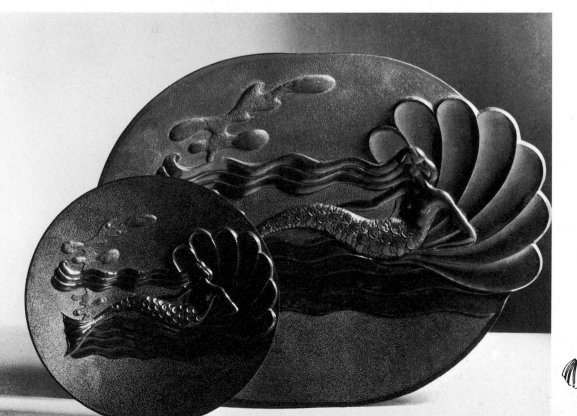

81

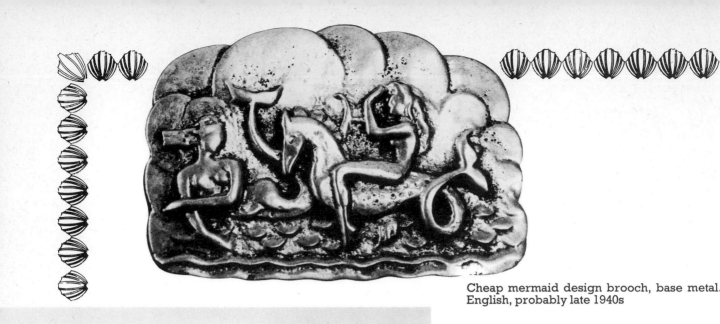

Cheap mermaid design brooch, base metal.
English, probably late 1940s

Sauce-boat with mermaid handle by Leslie
Durbin, 1955. It is customary for Royal
Academicians upon election to present to
the Royal Academy a piece of silver for the
use of their dining club. This piece was made
for presentation by Sir Hubert Worthington,
the architect

Publicity handout for the film *Miranda*, 1948

The mermaid swam into mainstream art in the *Sirenes* and *Nymphes des Eaux* by Paul Delvaux (b. 1907). A retrospective exhibition of Delvaux at the Palais des Beaux-Arts, Brussels, from 16 December 1944 to 14 January 1945 may have helped to spread the theme. He painted *Le Village des Sirenes* in 1942; *Composition, femmes devant le mer* (illustrated here) in 1943; and *Les grands sirenes* in 1947.[13]

A British film, *Miranda* (1948), described how a doctor (played by Griffith Jones) on holiday from his wife snags an amorous mermaid (Glynis Johns) while fishing. Marian Mahler MSIA designed a woven fabric for Edinburgh Weavers Ltd in 1949 with both mermaid and flying horse motifs within balloon shapes. An advertisement of the same year from *Cadre de la vie contemporaine* shows that J. Mercier of the boulevard Voltaire, Paris, was making bronze mermaid and triton bas-reliefs for interior decorators. Again in 1949, Hans Feibusch executed a mermaid-and-Neptune mural in Stic-B paint for the Beach Hotel, Littlehampton, of which the Hon. Lionel Brett ARIBA (now Lord Esher) was the architect. A scraper-board mermaid in a rain of stars was one of the illustrations by John O'Connor to *Departures* by E. L. Grant Watson (1948), published by Pléiades Books. The mermaid theme was still popular in the 1950s. The cover of *Lilliput* for August 1950, by Margaret Fitton, shows a mermaid sitting in a deckchair and knitting an enormous 'glove' for her tail. A clever cartoon inside the same issue is divided into three frames: an apparently normal man and woman smile at each other, their heads only showing as they bathe in the sea; then he registers consternation as she makes a dive for him and her mertail flips up;

Paul Delvaux, *Composition, femmes devant la mer*, oil on canvas. 105 × 166 cm (41½ × 65½ in.). Signed and dated 1958, Marlborough Fine Art, London

Mermaid and winged horse motifs on woven fabric designed by Marian Mahler for Edinburgh weavers Ltd, 1949

Advertisement for 'Pschitt' by Savignac 1952

finally, she looks crestfallen as he charges on to the beach, roaring with laughter – a lusty centaur. A mermaid brooch by Joseph and Pearce, in gold set with diamonds, is illustrated in E. D. S. Bradford's *Contemporary Jewellery and Silver Design* (1950). The mermaid was used for two such different posters (both of 1951) as Savignac's design for Pschitt, in France, and Jerzy Staniszkis's for the Polish Committee for Peace.[14] *Photoplay* magazine of 1 May 1957 illustrated the jewelled mermaids which decorated the hall of Debra Paget's 27-room Mediterranean-style mansion off Sunset Boulevard.[15] And in 1959 the Mermaid Theatre opened in London.

The finest *tour-de-force* of mermaidiana was in a competition of which the results were published in *Lilliput* in July 1955. Competitors were asked to complete the following limerick:

> King Neptune one day on the shore
> Was intrigued by a mermaid he saw.
> Said this jovial male:
> 'How I envy your tail –
>
> ....,'

The £5 winners suggested the following last lines:

> 'I find darning socks such a bore!'

> 'What a fish! What a dish in the raw!'

> 'Pass the salt, and don't ask me what for!'

> 'But, Glynis, it's you I adore!'

> 'But your ''flip''-pancy, dear, I deplore!'

There was even a demand for the Real Thing. In *The New Look* (1964), Harry Hopkins wrote of the year 1948:

> And yet uneasiness remained. There were still many moments in the late forties – as there were to be other, very different, moments in the fifties – when to many Englishmen this seemed an England they could scarcely recognise. Identity cards still had to be carried and shown at a policeman's demand. The streets were still drab, unpainted and dim-lit. In the West End, Oxford Street seemed to have become a succession of pin-table arcades and garish side-shows, offering such attractions as a REAL LIVE MERMAID IN A TANK OF GOLDFISH . . . .

The English Catalogue of Books records at least nine mermaid books for the years 1942–59[16] and there were also mermaid-decorated covers such as for Eileen Molony's *The Mermaid of Zennor* (1946), and the Grey Walls Press selection of Christopher Smart's poems, which was edited by the William Blake enthusiast and forties 'character', Ruthven Todd (1947).[17] Mermaids were also being constantly illustrated in *The Saturday Book*, founded in 1940, which, because it had no political animus or social message, became a kind of sampling-flask of the English unconscious. Like fairy tales, where equally there is no pressure on the author to include or omit anything (except to omit the overtly pornographic), *The Saturday Book* is a fair sample; and as with fairy tales, what was originally intended only to divert can now be analysed for deeper, latent meaning.[18]

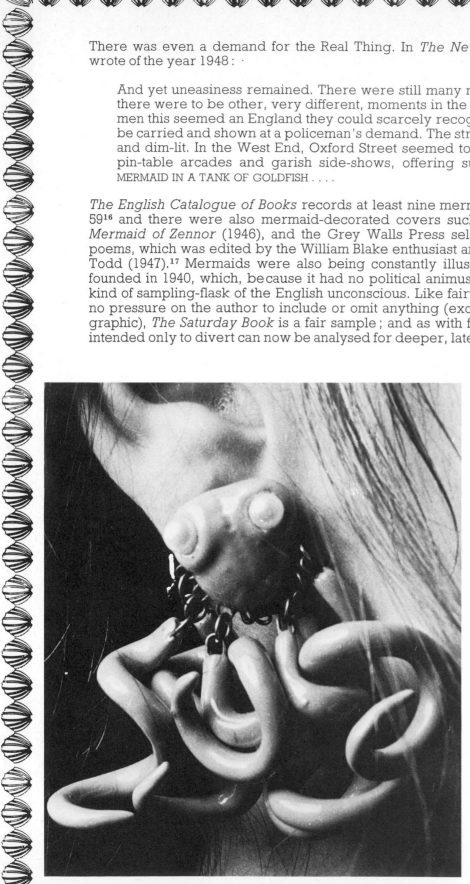

Octopus earring, late 1940s. Plastic, metal and synthetic pearls. Marie Middleton

It is possible, I suppose, that the mermaid motif is the emblem of some mass psychological fixation which escapes me: Edward Lucie-Smith has suggested that the mermaid's large fishtail 'can be thought of as a gigantic penis, stolen by the woman who forms the creature's upper half'. I prefer to think, more simply, that their mythological status gave mermaids an escapist charm, opposed to the mortal terrors so recently offered by the sea – a contrast made explicit by Charles Madge in 'The Mermaid' and by T.S. Eliot in 'The Love Song of J. Alfred Prufrock', who had 'heard the mermaids singing, each to each':

> We have lingered in the chambers of the sea
> By sea-girls wreathed with seaweed red and brown
> Till human voices wake us, and we drown.

The mermaid was the most frequent sea motif; but the sea, seaside and slimy things from the deep were generally popular in post-war design. Jean Lurçat's lyrical tapestry, *Le Chant de la mer,* was woven by the Atelier Jansen in 1948. Canvas artists such as Tristram Hillier, Edward Wadsworth, and Tunnard were best known for sea-shore scenes: as if they had taken to heart the injunction in the first stanza of Eliot's 'Sweeney Erect':

> Paint me a cavernous waste shore
> Cast in the unstilled Cyclades,
> Paint me the bold anfractuous rocks
> Faced by the snarled and yelping seas.

For the ballet *Miracle in the Gorbals,* Edward Burra painted a dropscene showing the towering chained hull of a ship in dry dock, against a rain-laden sky pierced by vast cranes; and Bliss incorporated a wailing ship's siren into the music. Advertisers introduced sea imagery to give their products appeal: Andrews Liver Salt 'To *keep* your seaside sprightliness' (*John Bull,* 21 July 1951); tropical fish to sell Imperial Leather soap (*Lilliput,* January 1949); and 'Seven Seas' – 'the sea-fresh vitamin food', the brand name tattooed on the chest of a husky matelot (*Modern Publicity,* 1951–52). Holbrook's Worcestershire Sauce issued *Annie the Anchovy* as their 'book of the year' for children in 1947, with illustrations by Win Roberts such as 'Seahorses, drawing the ceremonial scallop'. The enthralled children who received a copy would be sent 'skimming over the seven seas in search of the 27 ingredients that go to the making of Holbrook's Worcestershire Sauce'.

In 1956 Vicke Lindstrand designed a vase called 'Atlantis' for the AB Kosta Glasbruk, Sweden; the design, cut in clear crystal, was of shoals of small fish against a background of nets embodied in the glass. The plastic 'Dreamlight' lamp shown here, with its waving shape and seaweed-like markings, seems to me as fine an example of forties popular design as one could find. The plastic octopus earring represents the kitsch end of the same market.

The seaside meant holidays, of which everyone was in need. One must remember, too, that the sea shores had been forbidden territory in the war, and were only now being opened to the public again. Christopher Marsden, in *The English at the Seaside* (1947), catches brilliantly what this meant to people at the time:

> All round the southern and eastern shores of England the concrete has been broken up and the wire pulled down. The gaping holes in the piers which used to carry our August merriment into mid-Channel have gradually been filled in. Here and there, a rare explosion still announces the detonation of a mine. But already from Crescents, Terraces and Parades, from bow-fronted Regency villas and craggy Victorian chalets, we can scan once more the English and St George's Channels, the North Sea and the Atlantic Ocean. Soon our coastline will be clear again from Berwick to Dungeness, from Rye to Penzance, from St Ives to Silloth.

Edward Burra's design for drop-scene in the Helpmann-Bliss ballet *Miracle in the Gorbals*, 1944

Dedication page from T. A. Stephenson's *Seashore Life and Pattern.* Dedication reads 'To my Wife'

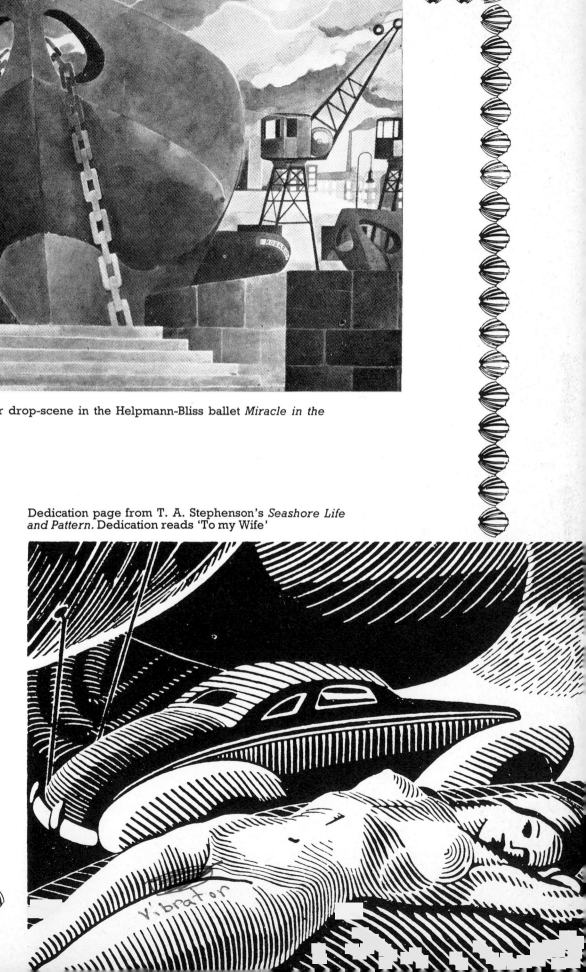

astic vase, stamped
reamlight' English 1940s

The English can resume, where they will, their odd littoral enjoyments. Once again they will be able to fill their hair with salt and their shoes with stones; they will be free once more to migrate to small and rainy towns in trains that are only crowded at the very time they travel; to leave their comfortable homes to eat unlovely meals in lodgings presided over by cross women of fanatical parsimoniousness. . . . The more reasonable sensual pleasures of the seaside will also be open to them: the wriggling of bare toes in sand; the working of depressions for buttocks; the popping of blistered seaweed. They will be able to inhale again in the sunshine that curious aroma, always slightly fecal, which belongs to the rearward part of beaches – composed of flies and old newspapers and unintentionally dried fish.

John Betjeman's 'Beside the Seaside' and 'North Coast Recollections', full of squelching bladderwrack, tamarisk, pebbly backwash and shrivelled seapinks, appeared in his *Selected Poems* in 1948; in 'Margate 1940', which appeared in *New Bats in Old Belfries* (1945), he had recalled the pre-war delights of that 'salt-scented town', ending the poem:

> And I think, as the fairy-lit sights I recall,
> It is those we are fighting for, foremost of all.

Professor T. A. Stephenson's *Seashore Life and Pattern,* which has the most extraordinary dedication page of any book ever published, appeared in 1944. In 1940, when that quaint, attractive coin (now defunct), the twelve-sided threepenny bit, was introduced, the Government, indulging in a rather heavy pun, approved a design of which one side showed the seashore flower, thrift.[19]

A tempting view of Middleton Tower Holiday Camp in 1954

Middleton Tower Holiday Camp

Publicity advertisement for the film *Theirs is the Glory* in the *Daily Film Renter*, 8 August 1946

Winged horses

Just as the mermaid symbolized the new freedom of the seas, the winged horse represented the new safety of the air. The lyrical Pegasus of classical legend took over from the Horse-men of the Apocalypse, who were represented on an advertisement for the film *Theirs is the Glory* in 1946. The new flying horse was celebrated by C. Day Lewis in his 1957 book, *Pegasus and Other Poems.* Its eponymous poem contained the lines :

> It was there on the hillside, no tall traveller's story.
> A cloud caught on a whin-bush, an airing of bleached
> Linen, a swan, the cliff of a marble quarry –
> It could have been any of these : but as he approached,
> He saw that it was indeed what he had cause
> Both to doubt and believe in – a horse, a winged white horse. . . .
>
> It stood there, solid as ivory, dreamy as smoke ;
> Or moved, and its hooves went dewdropping so lightly
> That even the wild cyclamen were not broken :
> But when those hooves struck rock, such was their might
> They tapped a crystal vein which flowed into song
> As it ran through thyme and grasses down-along.
>
> 'Pegasus,' he called, 'Pegasus' – with the surprise
> Of one who for the first time naming his naked lover.
> The creature turned its lordly, incurious eyes
> Upon the young man ; but they seemed to pass him over
> As something beneath their pride or beyond their ken.
> It returned to cropping the violets and cyclamen.

Winged horse in porcelain, *c.* 1950. Marked 'Wade porcelain made in England'

Francis Berry's book of poems, *The Galloping Centaur*, was published in 1952 by Methuen; and John Bowen, whose *The Mermaid and the Boy* was published in 1958, also wrote *Pegasus* (Faber & Faber, 1957).

Winged horses appear in an advertisement for the film *The Thief of Bagdad,* and are almost exactly paralleled by a Wade porcelain model. A play by Beresford Egan (better known as an artist), performed at the Watergate Theatre, London, from 21 March until 2 April, 1950, with John Longden in the leading role, was called *No Flies on Pegasus.* In Jerry Shelton's story 'Devils from Darkonia' in the American *Fantastic Story Magazine* of May 1953 a squadron of winged horses invades a professor's study. The New York night-club to which Frankie Christopher (Victor Mature) takes Jill Lynn (Betty Grable) in Bruce Humberstone's film *Hot Spot* (1941) is the Pegasus Club, with a large ceramic winged horse as the central motif of the interior décor. And splendid wood-engravings which John Buckland-Wright executed between 1943 and 1947 for the Golden Cockerel Press edition of Keats's 'Endymion' included a scene of riders on winged horses swooping through the empyrean.

In 1951 A. Gallmann of Zurich used the winged horse motif to advertise his publicity agency, with this caption:

> According to Greek mythology, Pegasus once revealed a spring consecrated to the Muses, by a blow from his hoof. This happened on Mount Olympus, where he lived in the Temple of Zeus and drew his chariot of thunder and lightning.
>
> From that day onwards, Muses, poets and writers drew their inspiration from this source. They came to the spring to enhance their intellectual powers when they wanted to write poetically or to convince their readers with bewitching words. It was the source of their wit.
>
> Many centuries later Pegasus was used as a symbol in ancient Corinth, a flourishing city whose prosperity was founded in seafaring and the arts.
>
> So you can see why I have two reasons for choosing this symbol for my work.[20]

'The winged horses cantered about among the professor's papers'. Illustration to story 'Devils from Darkonia' by Jerry Shelton, *Fantastic Story Magazine*, USA May 1953

Cheap plastic winged horse brooches, English early 1950s. Anton and Susan Marsh

It is significant that the winged horse had also been a popular motif in the insouciant 1920s which followed the First World War: two good examples were illustrated in *Die Kunst* of 1927, a porcelain example modelled by Arthur Storch for the Alteste Volkstedter Porzellanfabrik, and a blown glass one, incorporated into an elaborate air-twist glass candelabrum, made by J. Berger for the Bimini-Werkstätten, Vienna.

The Pegasus motif can also be attributed to a general escapist interest in classical mythology after the Second World War, comparable with the interest in Pre-Columbian mythology after the Great War, when Mexico became the escapist's paradise. We have already seen a centaur paired off with a mermaid in a *Lilliput* cartoon. He appears also in

Anonymous mythical group. Pottery with heavy white glaze, *c*. 1950 probably English.

Jean Carlu's 1951 poster for Cinzano[21] and again, holding a child, as the emblem of the British Council for Health Education in the same year, in a design by Kenneth Bromfield.[22] Most absurdly, he turns up in a 1947 advertisement for Cusson's Lipstick, painting the lips of a marble woman's head which rests against the fluting of a Grecian column.[23]

John Hutton designed a 'Perseus' panel, worked with brilliant-cutting, engraving, acid embossing and sandblasting, for the unromantically named London Sand Blast Decorative Glass Works in 1948.[24] A head of Mercury advertised the C. J. Palm Advertising Agency, Amsterdam, in 1951[25] and in the same year a two-headed Janus advertised Pimm's No. 1 ('The most heavenly drink in the world'): 'What a lucky god that fellow is, to be able to enjoy two Pimms at once.'[26] Hilda Durkin designed a 50-inch screen-printed chintz for Warner and Sons, Ltd. (Great Britain) entitled 'Pygmalion'.[27] Potters found classical themes particularly congenial. Bode Willumsen's group 'The Brave Tailor', modelled in stoneware for the Royal Copenhagen Porcelain Factory, showed a tailor clinging to the branch of a tree in which a unicorn has embedded its horn.[28] Stig Lindberg made a stoneware figure of Daphne turning into a tree, for Gustavberg's Studio in 1949.[29] William Newland, a British modeller, made 'Minoan Bull' in 1954,[30] though the chunky design in red clay with trailed slip decoration had more in common with eighteenth-century Staffordshire wares than with those of ancient Crete.

A devastating war encourages men's superstitious instincts, and perhaps this, too, is a partial explanation of the myth revival of the forties and early fifties. In *Walking With Fancy* (1943), E. L. Grant Watson shows how superstition could seize the mind of a twentieth-century man:

> Under the influence of war I have come nearer to the normal life of the peasant; that life which has been lived by the vast majority of men for hundreds of generations. The cultivation of the soil, even on a small scale, involves the keeping of animals, and the keeping of animals involves, sooner or later, the killing of them. . . . After the killing there follows the taking out of the bowels, and in the course of the war months I have become familiar with those parts of animals which are usually hidden: the guts, the innards, the secret paraphernalia of their metamorphosis, the *penetralia* in fact, which to the peoples of the ancient world were associated with a deep sense of awe and wonder. Certainly the movements of the viscera after death are arresting and peculiar, and it is easy to understand how these automatic contractions and expansions should have stirred the imaginations of the early races of mankind who shared a mystical participation with all living things.

Among canvas painters of the period for whom classical mythology provided many subjects, one might single out Karl Rössing, whose works have become better known through a comprehensive retrospective exhibition at Nuremburg in 1973. The same influence is seen in the fifties drawings of the English painter and sculptor William Redgrave, and generally in the Romantic Revival school led by John Piper and Graham Sutherland.

Balloons

The first two lines of Wordsworth's poem 'Peter Bell' are:

> There's something in a flying horse
> There's something in a huge balloon.

A neat juxtaposition of two of the prime images of post-Second World War design. Like the flying horse, the balloon symbolized the new freedom of the skies. A clear example of the Oyster Principle in action, it represented the parachute in masquerade – replacing something plain and menacing which dropped from the skies to the earth, by something gay and fanciful which rose from the earth to the skies. And, more obviously, it was a friendly replacement for the barrage balloon. It is significant that in 1947, the year of the New Look, Elsa Schiaparelli held a Balloon Ball. This is how she describes it (writing in the third person) in her memoirs:

> The invitation cards were shaped like the famous balloon of the Montgolfier brothers in the eighteenth century, and guests were asked to wear these cards as badges at the entrance. There was, oddly enough, a club of balloon enthusiasts who still made almost daily ascents, floating at the mercy of the winds, and Schiap succeeded in hiring for the evening the largest of these balloons which, duly inflated, she placed in the middle of the garden, which it covered like a roof. In the basket sat a man who looked strangely like M. Picard, the balloonist and deep-sea diver. Perhaps it was M. Picard incognito! Green and pink lights played between the trees, and the tables were covered with shocking tarlatan. People coming in through the courtyard, looking through the windows of the house into the distant garden, had the impression of an immense grey elephant bathed in a rainbow. They asked how Schiap had captured him, not realizing that a balloon when deflated can slip through anything.
> It was a wonderful evening. The women sparkled and shimmered as on pre-war nights. Maharajahs and their wives added to the beauty of the scene. It was a gesture of defiance against the hard years we were just pulling out of, and an augury of what the future would be.

In the same year, the *Contact* book *World Off Duty* made liberal use of balloon motifs designed by Edward Bawden; a striking balloon cover had already appeared on *Lilliput* in May 1945.

Advertisers, as usual, were quick to exploit the new fashion: the House of Saville used a brilliantly coloured balloon design in 1948 to advertise their services, while Philips in the same year showed radio valves ascending into the sky like balloons.

A dining recess designed by Josef Frank for Svenskt Tenn contained a hanging lamp just like a balloon in flight. Charles Gibbs-Smith's King Penguin on *Ballooning* appeared in 1949 with a fetching cover designed by Marian Mahler MSIA, characteristically showing carousel figures and swing-boats hanging from balloons.

William Pène du Bois's children's book, *The Twenty-One Balloons* (already mentioned) was published by Robert Hale in 1949 and won the Newberry Prize in America for the year's 'most distinguished contribution to literature for children'. William du Bois was thirty-three in 1949; his previous books included *The Great Geppy* (1940), a tale of a red and white striped horse who was a detective at a circus. During the war he had served with the artillery in Bermuda and found time to publish a lively army newspaper which

Title page of *Contact* 6, 1947, designed by Edward Bawden

A CONTACT BOOK

CONTACT PUBLICATIONS LIMITED 26 MANCHESTER SQUARE LONDON W1

Glamorizing a product by showing it as a 'balloon' advertisement for Philips, Sweden, valves, by Inga-Greta Solbreck-Moller, 1948

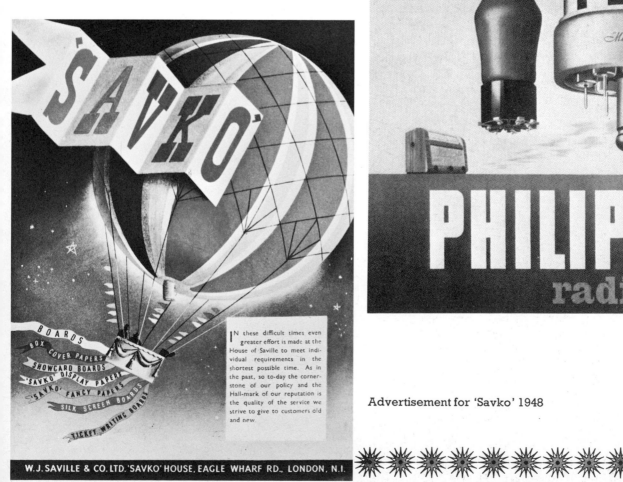

IN these difficult times even greater effort is made at the House of Saville to meet individual requirements in the shortest possible time. As in the past, so to-day the corner-stone of our policy and the Hall-mark of our reputation is the quality of the service we strive to give to customers old and new.

W. J. SAVILLE & CO. LTD. 'SAVKO' HOUSE, EAGLE WHARF RD., LONDON, N.I.

Advertisement for 'Savko' 1948

Lampshade in the form of a balloon in dining recess designed by Josef Frank for Svenskt Tenn, 1948

won an overseas camp newspaper prize. Frank Wilson's novel, *Mike the Muckshufter* (1946), included a balloon race round the Isle of Wight by Professor Pommes de Terre and M. Vol-à-vent (*sic*).

The balloon motif became even more popular in the 1950s. In 1950 Four Roses whiskey advertised a glass of their product floating heavenwards in a balloon basket with four dew-dappled rose blooms. A Captain and Mrs McCoy and family so far forgot their Salvation Army propriety as to show themselves in their uniforms on their Christmas card that year floating in balloons held by a jovial Father Christmas. Another hanging lamp in the form of a balloon, made from thin perforated slats of polished beech plywood, was designed by E. R. Aldhouse MSIA for Primavera. An outsize Outspan orange was converted into a balloon in an advertisement in *John Bull*, 27 August 1955. Terence Conran designed balloon motifs in yellow, pink, blue and green to decorate white earthenware tableware by Conran Ceramics in 1956.

White earthenware tableware, designed by Terence Conran, and made by Conran Ceramics Great Britain

Advertisement for Outspan oranges, *John Bull*, 27 August 1955

O for OUTSPAN

the tonic that's a treat

So good to eat . . . they're fresh and sweet, packed with luscious juices! Get some today and *prove* it!

So good for you . . . vitamins are delicate things but nature captures them from the hot South African sun and makes each Outspan *extra* rich in vitamin C. When they're ripe, Outspan are sealed so that they stay fresh and full of goodness right up to the moment you eat them. The *freshest* vitamin C and stimulating sugars make Outspan the best of all pick-me-ups for any time of day.

Outspan

Britain's favourite orange

And grapefruit, too!—have them for breakfast. They make the freshest start to every day!

Here's an easy Outspan recipe

Orange Cream

1 small tin evaporated milk
1 packet orange jelly (1 pint)
4 Outspan Oranges
2-3 tablespoonfuls caster sugar

Place unopened tin of milk in water and boil 10 minutes. Cool. Dissolve jelly in 1 pint water. Make up to 1 pint with juice of 2 oranges and water. Whip evaporated milk till thick and add cooled jelly, sugar, and grated orange rind. Whisk and pour into sundae glasses. Decorate with orange segments.

Worth reaching for

If you're one of the many, many people who'd rather drink Four Roses, you'll find it well worth reaching for. It gives you so much more in quality for so little more in price.

Wouldn't you *rather* drink **FOUR ROSES**?

Again a product glamorized by association with a balloon: advertisement for Four Roses whiskey, designed by Anton Bruehl, 1950

99

'Old Stagers', 50-inch Rosebank printed cotton with design of balloons, 'Old crock' motor cars, penny-farthing bicycles and antiquated locomotives, 1957

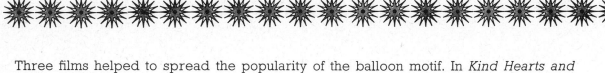

Three films helped to spread the popularity of the balloon motif. In *Kind Hearts and Coronets* (1949), Lady Agatha d'Ascoyne (one of the many roles played in the film by Alec Guinness) distributes leaflets from a balloon after her release from Holloway for suffragette activities, and is shot down by Louis Mazzini (Dennis Price) with a bow and arrow. Michael Todd's extravaganza, *Around the World in Eighty Days*, was screened in 1956 – the year in which Mary Quant designed her 'Balloon Dress'. David Niven, who played the globe-encircling Phineas Fogg (sharing his balloon with Cantinflas as Passepartout), would later call his autobiography *The Moon's a Balloon. The Red Balloon* (1956), directed by Albert Lamorisse, was a winsome picture about a boy with a balloon on a string.

The balloon theme was still going strong in 1961, when Allen and Unwin published *Trip in a Balloon*, a picture-book of another film, *Le Voyage en Ballon*, by Albert Lamorisse. And in 1964 Collins published René Guillot's *Balloon Journey* with an attractive pictorial jacket designed by David Knight.

Illustration from *The Twenty-One Balloons*, written and illustrated by William Pène du Bois, 1949

Heraldry

Heraldry might be considered the folk art of the aristocracy. As already suggested, its popularity with forties and fifties designers can be explained as another working-out of the Oyster Principle, an attempt to make friendly the badges and symbols of war. In 1953 there was the additional heraldic allure of a Coronation. Among the other Coronation literature, a book was issued on heraldic symbols, called *The Queen's Beasts.* H. Stanford London, Norfolk Herald Extraordinary, wrote the descriptions; there were a foreword by the Hon. Sir George Bellew, Garter King of Arms, splendid colour illustrations by Edward Bawden and Cecil Keeling, and photographic reproductions of the heraldic figures sculptured for the Coronation by James Woodford.

But there was another reason that brought heraldry into favour after the turmoil and disruption of war. Geoffrey Grigson, a poet and critic pure, concrete and abrasive as cuttlefish bone, who stood as a sort of Ruskin to the 1940s,[31] called his 1950 autobiography *The Crest on the Silver,* and one passage in it goes a long way to explain the appeal of blazoned genealogy after the Second World War:

Cover of G. E. Pallant Sidaway's *Signs and Symbols*, 1952

Heraldic medallion designed by Marcel Renard, 1949 for Cie Gle. Transatlantique, 'Ile de France', French Line

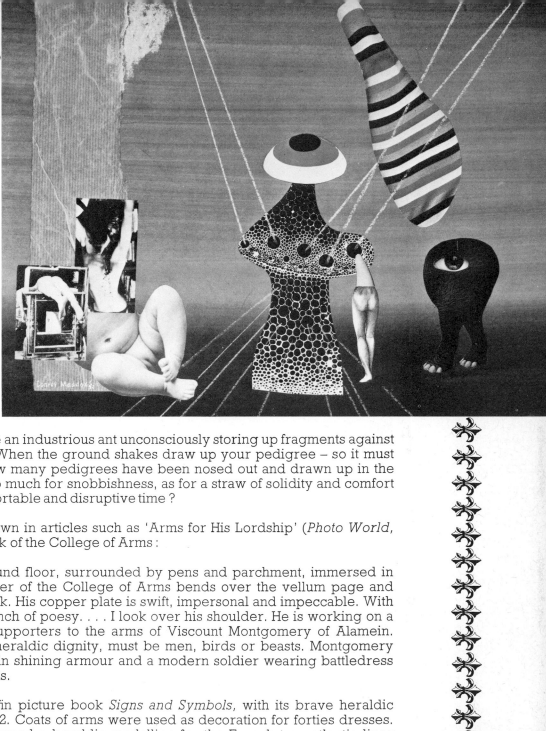

Conroy Maddox *Heraldry of the Family*, collage 1952. 32 × 43cm (12⅝ × 16⅞in). Signed and dated. Hamet Gallery

My grandfather was like an industrious ant unconsciously storing up fragments against the ruin of his world. When the ground shakes draw up your pedigree – so it must have been felt; and how many pedigrees have been nosed out and drawn up in the last eighty years, not so much for snobbishness, as for a straw of solidity and comfort to grasp at in an uncomfortable and disruptive time?

Interest in heraldry was shown in articles such as 'Arms for His Lordship' (*Photo World*, October 1946) about the work of the College of Arms:

At his desk on the ground floor, surrounded by pens and parchment, immersed in monkish calm, the Writer of the College of Arms bends over the vellum page and dips his pen in Indian ink. His copper plate is swift, impersonal and impeccable. With him pothooks are a branch of poesy. . . . I look over his shoulder. He is working on a Patent which assigns supporters to the arms of Viscount Montgomery of Alamein. Supporters, an added heraldic dignity, must be men, birds or beasts. Montgomery has chosen a crusader in shining armour and a modern soldier wearing battledress and the beret of the tanks.

G. E. Pallant Sidaway's Puffin picture book *Signs and Symbols,* with its brave heraldic cover, was published in 1952. Coats of arms were used as decoration for forties dresses. In 1949 Marcel Renard designed a heraldic medallion for the French transatlantic liner Ile de France. In 1952 Conroy Maddox, the English surrealist, entitled one of his oddest works, for no immediately apparent reason, *Heraldry of the Family.* In 1953, Coronation year, Peggy Tearle designed and made a heraldic lion and unicorn in peccary and gold kid with jewelled crown and coronet of silver gilt. In the same year Philip Stockford designed for Rosebank furnishing fabrics (manufactured by Turnbull and Stockdale of Ramsbottom, Manchester) 'Pomp and Circumstance', to be used on satin or linen, depicting the regalia and the insignia of the Orders of Chivalry. In 1958 Gluck, best known for her Art Deco paintings of the 1920s, portrayed Lord Justice Salmon, at the summing-up of the Liberace libel case, in front of a huge panel of the royal coat of arms. Another Art Deco designer, Erté, also gave himself over to fanciful heraldry in the fifties. Herbert Spencer MSIA, designed for Marconi's Wireless Telegraph Company a comic heraldic trade mark – a rampant lion brandishing a spanner and wrench.

Ertè, heraldic stage design of the early 1950s

Dress with heraldic design, 1940s Vernon
Lambert

Jacket designed by William Pène du Bois, for his book *The Twenty-One Balloons*, London 1949

Endpapers designed by John Minton for *Points of Contact*, London 1947. The influence of Samuel Palmer is strong

REFLECTIONS

REPORTS REVIEWS

Preoccupation with a clothing shortage

Out into the abysmal landscape of the subconscious, lonely stored with six years of no-clothes, the man-mind seeks the elementary basis of dress sufficiency among the confused synthesis of many needs and few clothing coupons. Even the normal coefficients of elasticity are lost in the spatial relationships of one shirt to some trousers in juxtaposition to the jacket of reality, and the stud of the present pins down the collar of scarcity.

Doctor, is there an Austin Reed in the house?

Escapist Art

In a book of 1948 sourly entitled *The End of an Age,* the ancient Dean Inge (it was certainly the end of *his* age) suggested that escapism was one of the evils of the time.[32] It was a fairly natural evil: there had been and still was quite a lot that it was reasonable to want to escape from. The main kind of escapism Inge singled out was surrealism. Surrealism was the great artistic fashion of the 1930s. As Peyton Skipwith has recently pointed out in an article in *The Connoisseur* (March 1974) it put out of fashion the fine naturalistic work of artists such as Ethelbert White, and encouraged artists who might have produced creditable naturalistic work to become indifferent surrealists. Some of the clichés of surrealism entered design and decorative art. This borrowing ranged from the outright comic parody, as in the Austin Reed advertisement in *Contact* 1947, with its Daliesque crutches, through the equally Daliesque distortions of F. F. Kern's sculpted walnut table with lucite top for Laszlo, Inc. of 1953, to the more discreet absorption of surrealist style in the use of isolated motifs with strong shadows on the book-jackets for Lillian Smith's *Strange Fruit* (1945, jacket design by Hans Tisdall), Katherine Everett's *Bricks and Flowers* (1949) and Douglas Reed's *Reasons of Health* (also 1949).

During the war, French surrealists were prominent in the resistance to dictatorship, which represented the enforcement of ideological uniformity – the antithesis of what surrealism stood for. Emerging from their hiding-places after the war, they organized in 1947 an International Post-War Exhibition of Surrealism. Frederick Kiesler, who in 1926 was demanding 'Vital Architecture' and the 'Space City', collaborated with Max Ernst, Miró, Matta, Duchamp and others to produce a 'Hall of Superstition', an ostentatious rejection of Bauhaus functionalism and a witty way of proving that buildings could be more than machines for living in. Kiesler wrote a manifesto for the 1947 exhibition, 'Magical Architecture':

Wall table with free-form clear Lucite top, on base of sculptured walnut, natural finish Designed by Paul Laszlo, sculpture by F. F. Kern, made by Laszlo Inc. (USA)

left
pastiche of Salvador Dali in an advertisement for Austin Reed,
Contact 1947

Six American ties of the 1940s, bought by the author at the fleamarket in Englishtown,
New Jersey, for 10 cents each, in 1970

Triang clockwork toy, mother and pram, 1950

Jacket designed by H. Cowdell
for Sir Osbert Sitwell's *The Death
of a God*, London, 1949

Page from *Contact 6*, 1947,
designed by Edward Bawden

109

'Modern functionalism' in architecture is dead. In so far as the 'function' was a survival – without even an examination of the Kingdom of the Body upon which it rested – it came to grief and was exhausted in the mystique hygiene plus aestheticism. (The Bauhaus, Corbusier's system, etc.)[33]

This rejection of the antiseptic functionalism of the twenties and thirties is central to the development of the decorative arts and architecture in the forties and fifties. The new philosophy was re-enunciated by the Viennese painter Hundertwasser (b. 1928) in July 1958 when he read his *Verschimmelungs-Manifest* (Mould Manifesto) in the Abbey of Seckau:

The material uninhabitability of the slums is preferable to the moral uninhabitability of functional, utilitarian architecture. In the so-called slums only man's body can perish, but in the architecture ostensibly planned for man, his soul perishes. . . . Functional architecture has proved to be a wrong road, just like painting with a ruler. With giant strides we are approaching impractical, unusable, and finally uninhabitable architecture.[34]

Hundertwasser had already made his point, less extravagantly, in an exhibition pamphlet aimed against 'the 90-degree angles of Vienna':

In 1920 the pavement and the walls of the houses had to be constructed smooth, but in 1957 this is an insanity I cannot understand. The air raids of 1943 were a perfect automatic lesson in form: straight lines and their vacuous structures ought to have been blown to pieces, and so they were. Following this a transautomatism ought normally to have occurred. . . . But we are building cubes, cubes! Where is our conscience?[35]

Another form of forties escapism was Gothick fantasy. Ruins, follies and ghosts were part of the happy old England,[36] and part of the stock-in-trade of the new romantic movement in painting led by John Piper and Graham Sutherland. Piper designed a fine Gothic jacket for the first edition of Henry Green's *Loving* (1945).The jacket of Edith Pargeter's *Lost Children* is also oppressively Gothick. The opening of Edith Pargeter's book (published by Heinemann, London 1951) revels in Gothicism, and relates it to the dynastic stability of the *ancien regime*:

Rose's Folly covers the highest rocky outcrop of the heathland as the cloud covers Table Mountain, sagging, wallowing, permanent, and yet for ever quivering and changing to the varying lights of day and evening. . . . All round it for miles the warrens and coppices and rolling wilderness of the Rose estates fend off the rest of the world; the woods depleted, the edges nibbled away by fields, but the encroaching sea of reality still held fast from over-running it by something of willpower, more of luck, and most of all by the sheer weight of habit and security of possession. As it was in the beginning, is now, and ever shall be, world without end, Amen! . . .

The railway line between Crocksford and Bredington, one of the earliest in England, skirts the estate and looks up across the lightly lifting miles of heath to a watch-tower placed high between fits of woodland, to suggest the fourteenth century, though it belongs to the nineteenth. Distance makes almost beautiful the shifting levels of land, bluish-black churning of trees and light-play of grasses, from which the house

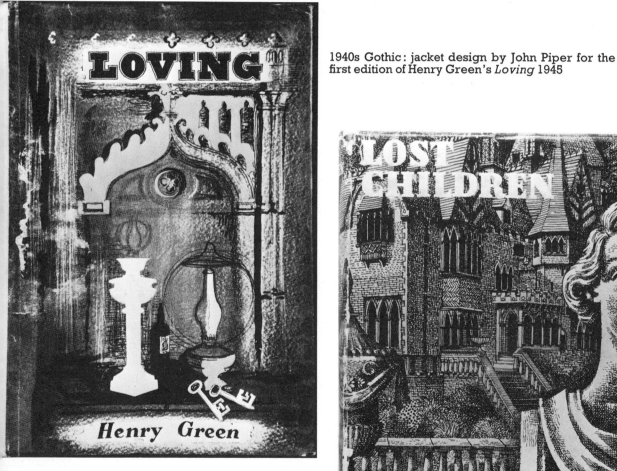

Pen and ink illustration by John Farleigh for *Haunted England*

1940s Gothic: jacket design by John Piper for the first edition of Henry Green's *Loving* 1945

Gothic: jacket design for Edith Pargeter's *Lost Children*, 1951

Glazed pottery coffee-set in the form of a palette with brushes, anon., c.1948. Michael and Gerlinde Costiff 35 × 30 cm (14 × 12 in.)

Dougie Field, oil painting in 1950s revival style, 1973. Collection of Dougie Field

emerges on its shallow table of rock. The crag is not high, so the Folly compensates with towers of improbable height and ferocity, shot with slit arrow-windows bordered with three-coloured brick of the railway age, slag blue, raw-clay-yellow and russet-red. Between the towers the complicated roofs run all ways in panic from their turreted Gothic corners, curly-crested, scalloped, battlemented to bewilderment, unsure of everything on earth but their own rightness and permanence. Every kind of window shuts out light from, rather than lets it into, the half miles of corridor and acres of hall within. You could get lost in the attics and wait days for a search-party. Among the twisted, towering, convoluted chimney-pots you could imagine yourself in a new Cheddar, laced with leaner stalagmites, and petrified from the beginning of the world. This monstrous erection, so huge that even across a waste of seven miles it seems to topple over you, ought to be self-conscious about its appearance; and what terrifies is that it sits there with no sense of guilt whatever, so assured, so fixed, so indifferent to your astonishment, that it achieves a formidable personality of its own. You are afraid even to shudder at it. For the truth is that Rose's Folly, for all its artificiality and newness, is only the latest facet of something old, genuine and immense, no more capable of awkwardness in this fresh guise than a woman in a new dress.

There have always been Roses. In the remote Norman and Saxon mists from which they came they do not smell any sweeter than the rest of their kind, perhaps, but they acquired the patina and the permanence of all antiques. . . .

I have quoted this passage at length because it encapsulates all the attitudes which made the Gothick attractive in the Austerity/Binge period. We are told that Rose's Folly was 'permanent'; that it is now 'as it was in the beginning'; later we are told that the Rose family have 'the permanence of all antiques'. Permanence was an attractive idea in a world where so much that had been considered permanent had been destroyed, from buildings to class attitudes and the servant hierarchy. It is seen as an advantage of the folly that 'the encroaching sea of reality' is kept at bay: escapism as the alternative to unpalatable reality. Finally, the folly is a facet of 'something old, genuine and immense': three qualities not to be found in the artefacts of Austerity/Binge, which were new, synthetic and small because smallness was economical and space-saving. The Gothick was also mysterious and romantic. To the same period belong John Piper's Strawberry Hill Gothick settings for Frederick Ashton's ballet *The Quest* (1943); a revival of the ballet *The Haunted Ballroom* at Sadler's Wells (1945); G. W. Stonier's *The Memoirs of a Ghost,* with jacket design by Eva Haman (1949); John Farleigh's pen-and-ink illustrations to *Haunted England* (1940); the Ealing Studios film *Dead of Night*, of which Leslie Hurry designed the poster; the Universal film *Phantom Lady* ('Watch out for her – she's no Phantom') starring Franchot Tone (1944); and a film adaptation of Sheridan Le Fanu's *Uncle Silas* (1947) with Derrick de Marney in the title role and Jean Simmons as Caroline Ruthyn.

This was also a favourable time for historical novels – the heyday of Heyer, whose preferred period was the English Regency. The American version of this kind of fantasy is well illustrated in the 1946 jacket to Joseph Hergesheimer's *Balisand.* During the First World War the absence of men had produced a cropped-hair and flat-chested look for women. The same conditions in the 1940s produced, at least in the theatre and cinema, a spate of women dressed in Regency top hats and tails: Merle Oberon as George Sand in the Columbia film about Chopin *A Song To Remember* (1944), and, on a lowlier level, Miss Burton of Miss Burton's School of Dancing, Redhill, Surrey, or Ouida Mary Holmes, the little black girl who in June 1940 was a silver medal winner at Audrey Mae Dumas's ninth annual dance revue in Xavier University Auditorium.

Ballet, the most escapist of all art forms, was in the throes of a renaissance in the 1940s. In *Ballet Since 1939*, a booklet published for the British Council in 1946, Arnold Haskell wrote: 'With the outbreak of war the demand for ballet steadily grew, partly no doubt

Forties Regency: Merle Oberon
as George Sand in the Columbia
Film *A Song to Remember*, 1945

Gothic: publicity handout for the
Universal film *Phantom Lady*, 1944

114

from escapism, since ballet is the last stronghold of theatrical illusion. . . .' Already in the 1930s the ballet in Britain had taken on a distinctively national character, and Haskell explains the stages by which this happened. The British ballet of the twentieth century was directly inspired by the Russian ballet imported by Diaghilev. Pavlova filled her company with English girls, who she found were as quick to learn as Russian ones, and more amenable to discipline, though English girls still had to take Russian names – Hilda Munnings, for example, became Lydia Sokolova – ballet, previously something to be sandwiched between the jugglers and the performing seals in the music hall, was now becoming a respectable accomplishment like the piano or violin. After the Russian Revolution, Diaghilev's supply of artists from Russia dried up, so he turned to Britain for such great artists as Vera Savina, Ninette de Valois, Alicia Markova and Anton Dolin. Diaghilev's death in 1929 left the way open for the development of a native British ballet. In 1930 P. J. S. Richardson, editor of the *Dancing Times*, and Arnold Haskell founded the Camargo Society, for giving ballet performances to subscription audiences four times a year. Edwin Evans, president of the Society for Contemporary Music, was chairman. Although the Camargo Society lasted only two years, it produced two major choreographers – Ninette de Valois and Frederick Ashton. The new English ballets it staged included *Job* (music by Vaughan Williams), *Pomona* and *Rio Grande* (music by Constant Lambert) and *Facade* (music by William Walton). It drew mainly on two studio groups – those of Marie Rambert and Ninette de Valois. Marie Rambert, who had come to the Russian ballet to

Televising a ballet: from *The Television Annual* 1952

Cover of the programme for Audrey Mae Dumas' ninth annual dance revue, Xavier University Auditorium, June 1940

Illustration from the programme of the June 1940 annual dance revue of Audrey Mae Dumas' school of dancing, in Xavier University Auditorium, USA

Compliments and Best Wishes to

My Little Girl

Ouida Mary Holmes

On Receiving Her Silver Ballet

Medal Tonight

★

With Love

FROM MOTHER

Page 10

OUIDA MARY HOLMES

A winning personality and a leader in her class. She will receive a silver medal for ballet dancing and a perfect attendance certificate.

Page 11

teach Nijinsky eurythmics, remained to learn classical ballet technique from Cecchetti. Her studio became a 'laboratory of talent'; by Diaghilev's death she had a group which included Pearl Argyle, Andrée Howard, Diana Gould, Prudence Hyman, William Chappell and Frederick Ashton. This company gave seasons at the Lyric, Hammersmith, and later on at her own Mercury Theatre. Ninette de Valois (*nee* Edris Stannus), a young Irish dancer, joined Diaghilev's ballet in 1923, and left to produce plays at two *avant-garde* theatres, the Abbey, Dublin, and the Festival, Cambridge. She formed her own choreographic group and in 1931 made her name with *Job,* an interpretation of the Bible story through the vision of William Blake. Blake and his follower Samuel Palmer were to be the main influences on British painting in general during the forties. Geoffrey Grigson's book on Palmer appeared in 1947, and Ruthven Todd's collection of poems *The Planet in My Hand* (1946) included no fewer than four poems on Blake and his followers: 'William Blake', 'Samuel Palmer at Reigate', 'Henry Fuseli' and 'Edward Calvert'.

With the co-operation of Lilian Baylis, the Sadler's Wells Ballet was formed; and Haskell's view is that 'British Ballet was born at Sadler's Wells when Alicia Markova (1935) withdrew to lead a company of her own.' Margot Fonteyn was growing to full stature as a ballerina at this time. In 1939 letters were written to the Press, including one by Bernard Shaw, suggesting that the few male dancers should be exempted from conscription. The Sadler's Wells management wisely refused to identify itself with this plea, and many of the male dancers joined up as volunteers or conscripts. The best-remembered wartime experience of the company was their goodwill tour of Holland in May 1940. They had just given their fourth performance at Arnhem when the Germans invaded. Their bus, a few hours ahead of the Panzers, reached the Hague in safety.

A series of ballets inspired by British subjects, authors or artists was produced in the war years. Ninette de Valois put on *The Rake's Progress,* the first Wells ballet with an English theme, in 1940 – interpreting Hogarth as she had Blake in *Job.* She also produced *The Prospect before Us* in 1940, a story of back-stage intrigue in late eighteenth-century London, inspired by Rowlandson drawings and with music by the eighteenth-century English composer William Boyce, selected by Constant Lambert. Although Frederick Ashton's first wartime production, *Dante Sonata,* was written in fury over the rape of Poland, its setting by Sophie Fedorovitch was based on the work of another school-of-Blake artist, Flaxman, well-known for his designs on Wedgwood ceramics. Another wartime work of Ashton's, produced during a special leave granted him for the purpose by the Air Ministry (he was an officer in the RAF) was based on a legend of St George from Spenser's *Faerie Queene.* The score was by Walton, the Gothick décor by Piper.

Robert Helpmann produced and danced in three British-inspired ballets: *Comus* (1942), *Hamlet* (1942) and *Miracle in the Gorbals* (1944). All three were given distinguished settings. *Comus,* a modification of an early English art form, the masque, was designed by Oliver Messel. *Miracle in the Gorbals,* as already stated, had a marine setting by Edward Burra. But for *Hamlet,* the young artist Leslie Hurry, 'discovered' by Helpmann at an exhibition of his work, designed perhaps the most overwhelming scenery ever visited on any ballet, a magnificent lowering composition dominated by a vengeful dagger-brandishing figure. With any dancer less striking than Helpmann, it could have stolen the show completely. While writing this book I visited Mr Hurry at his Suffolk cottage. He told me he was paid £15 for the designs – 'and then £5 extra because the ballet was a success'.

In the same year, Andrée Howard put on *Twelfth Night* with décor and costumes by Doris Zinkeisen; she had also been the choreographer for the ballet adaptation of David Garnett's fantasy *Lady into Fox,* presented by the Ballet Rambert in 1939 with décor and costumes by Nadia Benois. The ballet required the sudden metamorphosis of one of the characters, which was ingeniously achieved by a tail of ruffled muslin concealed in a Victorian bustle.

117

Robert Helpmann as Comus, 1942

Leslie Hurry's stage set for the
Helpmann ballet *Hamlet*

Balletomania was rampant in the forties. There was a good sale for Nicolas Bentley's amusing send-up of that phenomenon, *Ballet-Hoo* (first published 1937, revised edition published by Michael Joseph 1948) which described such celebrities as Serge Pantz, Irina Fallova and Michael Youpushoff. Arthur Sadler did a paper sculpture of *Les Syl-phides*.[37] Dancers and choreographers, with their autographs, were printed on a 'Jacqmar' headscarf, and Degas-like ballerinas on a skirt. Reproductions of Degas paintings hung in school corridors and art rooms.

Ballet became such a popular art form in the 1940s that a ballerina was even used to glamorize aluminium barrel containers: advertisement for John Dale Ltd, *Packaging and Display Encyclo-pedia 1948*

Skirt with ballerina motifs 1940s

Among the many books on ballet published in the forties [38] was a volume of *Paintings of the Ballet* (1947) by Theyre Lee-Elliott, who, among his other achievements, had been high-jump champion at Magdalene College, Cambridge, played lawn tennis for Cambridge University and table tennis for England, designed the British Air Mail symbol, the Imperial Airways speedbird symbol and the Post Office Telephone symbol, and executed the brilliant Art Deco book jackets to *Dodsworth, A Farewell to Arms, Juan in America*, Eugene Wright's *The Great Horn Spoon* and Francis Haskell's *Henry the Eighth*.[39] Lee-Elliott is a text-book example of the way in which decorative art was being released from the hard-edge geometry of Art Deco and indulging in a new balletic freedom, looseness and impressionism. Arnold Haskell wrote: 'It is not astonishing that Walt Disney, creator of the only true cinematographic ballet, should have become a great admirer of Lee-Elliott's work, presenting him with a study of Donald Duck, *Ballerina*.' The wonders of Disney were of course another escapist influence (though Disney also made animated propaganda films in wartime); these were the years of *Pinocchio, Fantasia* (1940), *Dumbo* (1941), *Bambi, Saludos Amigos* (1942), *The Three Caballeros* (1944), *Make Mine Music!, Song of the South* (1946), *Cinderella, The Adventures of Ichabod and Mr Toad, Slide, Donald, Slide* (1949), *Motor Mania* (1950), *Alice in Wonderland* (1951), *Peter Pan* (1953), *Lady and the Tramp* (1955) and *Sleeping Beauty* (1958), and also of many new films of Mickey Mouse, Donald Duck and the other 'silly symphony' characters. The basis of Disney's style was similar to that of Japanese prints in the late nineteenth century; flats of colour (in his case, often primary) within an uncompromising outline. In the history of art, Disney should also count as one of the great surrealists. Christopher Finch, in his new book on Disney, shows that an artist as distinguished as Charles Eames, the architect and furniture designer, was impressed by Disneyland.[40] And Mickey Mouse and his friends became popular decoration for crockery, clothes and (in transfers) furniture: these are among the most eagerly collected forties relics in America. Incidentally, I would like to take this chance of putting forward my doubtless seminal theory that Mickey's two round ears were originally based on the twin cases for the film reel on early cine-cameras.[41]

Other forms of escapism were the football pools, with their prospect of the mythopoeic £75,000 (the subject was commemorated by a film of 1948, *Easy Money*, starring Greta Gynt, Dennis Price and Jack Warner); and, of course fashion. In 1946 'Max Boy' published

Publicity handout for the Rank film *Easy Money* 1948

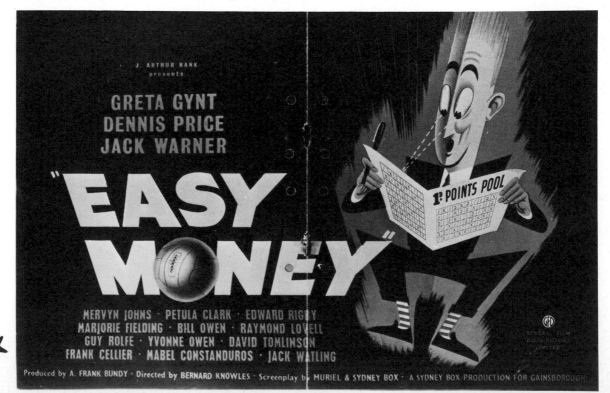

a book called *Modes and Mannequins,* which, the publishers claimed, 'enables every woman to witness a luxury parade of beautiful clothes, and to imagine herself wearing and displaying them before her friends.' As Sir William Darling wrote in his preface to the book:

> This writing is – first of all – just a little fiction for the coupon-starved ladies who are, nevertheless, still interested in clothes . . . during a period when most things are restricted or are in very short supply, a writing like this might be acceptable as a kind of solace for the ladies who cannot at present satisfy their desires for pretty things. . . . So I have spared nothing, and used as many yards of material as I desired without asking anyone's permission.

Hairstyles of the 1940s: from *Photo World* September 1946

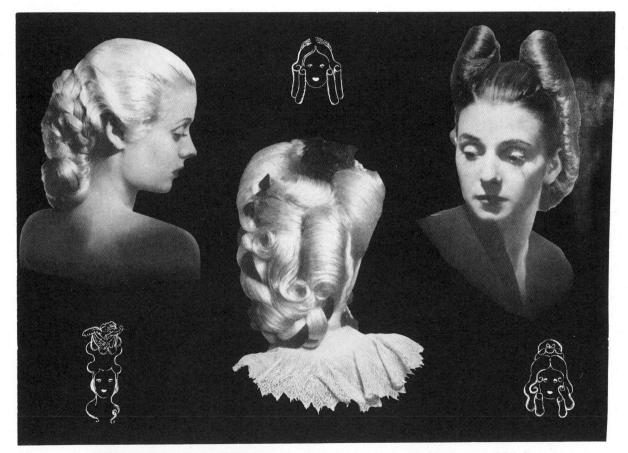

TREND IN TRESSES

THERE ARE MORE WAYS of dressing a woman's hair than mere man dreams of. Madame adapts her mode of hairdressing to the mood of the moment. During her lifetime she may range with the greatest of ease from eton crop, bingles, and bobs both long and short to "rolls," Edwardian styles.

Bouquets from the Army

ONE of the men we questioned was a Captain of Artillery (name deleted by military etiquette). He plunked for small hats...prefer, ably off-the-face. "When I'm out with a girl," said the gallant Captain, "I like to see her." straw sailor, cerise-ribboned: Gladys and Belle

1. Army or Navy beaux will approve this blue
2. High-visibility beret of emerald-green felt, with a pompon on top: Saks-Fifth Avenue
3. White surah back-of-head hat with purple knots. Helen Liebert; Bullock's-Wilshire
4. White piqué cotecomb hat trimmed with navy-blue grosgrain; Mary Goodfellow
5. For a pure brow—this Renoir bonnet of pale blue felt, cerise ribbon; Bonwit Teller
6. Molyneux's white organdie hat—its crown a rose. Made by Jeanne Tête; Bonwit Teller
7. White straw brim piped in navy-blue grosgrain, anchoring a navy-blue bow; Best
8. Swooping disk of pale pink felt, edged with pleated brown grosgrain; Erik of Paris
9. Fine stratagem—this hat of pink rosebuds, tiny green leaves; purple veil: Anna
10. Colonel's-lady toque of white raw silk, with streamers; Janet-Fifth Avenue; Ransohoff's
11. Navy-blue and white sailor, half felt, half braid; felt wing in back. Hodge hat; Altman
12. Sentimental blue ribbon and flowers, on a pink felt sailor. From Bertram Coppock
13. Mexican-dancer hat of natural Milan straw, black fish-net veiling and scarf; Fred Lacome

Special hats number,
Vogue, 1940s

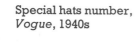

'Memories Pictures'
Leatherette cover of
1940s scrap album, USA

122

MEMOIRS · PICTURES

Carol Landis, leading lady of the Paramount wartime film *Mystery Sea
Raider*

Advertisement for Dolcis
shoes, Daily Mail Film
Award Annual 1947

J · ARTHUR RANK STARS
WEAR DOLCIS SHOES
The Star — Greta Gynt
Her shoes
distinctively
DOLCIS

Gloria James in the 1940s

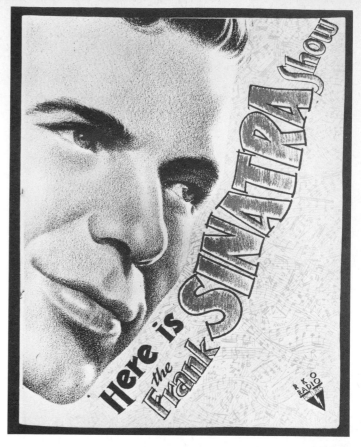

A male archetype of the 1940s: Frank Sinatra, from a film publicity handout

Cheap plastic jewellery of the 1940s
Marie Middleton

Right
Jacket of *Modes and Mannequins* by 'Max Boy' (Sir William Darling) 1946

Left
Judy Garland in *Summer Stock*, her last film for MGM, 1950

In 1947 the New Look arrived from Paris, with wasp waist, bustle, feminine curves and long swirling skirts. Harold Wilson, then President of the Board of Trade, appeared on film to condemn the waste of material. But in spite of killjoy protests at the 'hipettes' which were to be sold at 25s. 6d. a pair to pad out the dresses; in spite of frowns from Sir Stafford Cripps and fury from Miss Mabel Ridealgh, MP for North Ilford, who took the Women's Lib view that the fashion would once more give women that 'caged bird' look, the style triumphed. The squarish look of the war years gave place to rampant femininity. In the fifties men were also given the chance of fashion escapism in the 'Teddy Boy' style which, like the women's New Look, harked back to a rosier past; though in the gracious days of King Edward VII which the velvet-lapelled frock-coats were supposed to recall, most of the 'Teds' (or 'Greasers', as they were known in America) wearing them in the fifties would have been in service, with little money to splash about on fancy clothes.

The Fifties

19 51

THE FIFTIES

In 1950 it was enacted in Britain that practising witchcraft should no longer be an indictable offence. Warlocks and sibyls throughout the country breathed easier. The newts' eye trade boomed. In future, wands could be waved in public; wax images of one's neighbours, stuck with pins, could be hung in the window and the village hag could buy a besom without being interrogated by the police. This comic piece of legislation somehow symbolizes the spirit of the fifties – whimsical, superfluous, official but facetious, and marking the emergence of Britain from the Dark Ages.

It has often been pointed out that the character of the 1930s is fundamentally different from, if not the antithesis of, that of the 1920s. The twenties saw the reaction of the hectic, flapperish, Bright Young Things after the Great War; then, after the cesura of the 1929 Depression, there followed a grimmer decade, strongly politically conscious, in which the decorative arts became more uncompromisingly hard-edge and the new austere materials, plastic, sheet glass and chrome, were adopted generally instead of just in chic Parisian apartments. The 1940s and 1950s represent the same kind of antithesis, but in reverse: the war is followed by a grimly austere period, with Utility furniture; then comes the Binge of the fifties, with aggressive whimsy, frothy fashions, and the Rock culture – a division of decades neatly marked in Britain by the defiant carnival gesture of the Festival of Britain in 1951. Indeed, one might well say of the fifties what Tony Bouilhet said of the twenties:

'Ornament seemed to take a revenge on the inhuman times through which men had just passed.'

The Festival of Britain

In England the new spirit was put on parade at the Festival of Britain. This was something quite different from the 'Britain Can Make It' exhibition of 1946 (a dogged demonstration that Britain was not crushed and that she was getting to her feet again): it was a triumphant celebration of recovery and 'regeneration', neatly tied to the centenary of that other great chauvinist display of national designing talent, the Great Exhibition at Crystal Palace in 1851. The origin of the Festival was an open letter from Gerald Barry, Editor of the *News Chronicle,* to Sir Stafford Cripps (then President of the Board of Trade) on 14 September 1945:

Dear Sir Stafford Cripps,
        You have recently called upon the British people to re-establish their economic position in the world by their own exertions, and have drawn attention to the imperative need to stimulate British exports.
    May I urge the claims – as one means towards these essential needs – of a great Trade and Cultural Exhibition to be held in London within the next few years?
    It so happens that we are approaching a significant date. The year 1951 will see the centenary of the great and successful International Exhibition of 1851. . . .

King George VI and Queen Elizabeth with Gerald Barry, looking at a model of the Skylon on a visit to the Festival of Britain Office, Savoy Court, London, 2 May 1950

The Dome of Discovery and the Skylon, 1951

Progress on the South Bank: the Royal Festival Hall and the Shot Tower (now demolished) on 12 March 1951

The symbol of the Festival of Britain, designed by Abram Games

The Royal Suite and administrative accommodation, of 'fairground' appearance, being built on 15 February 1951

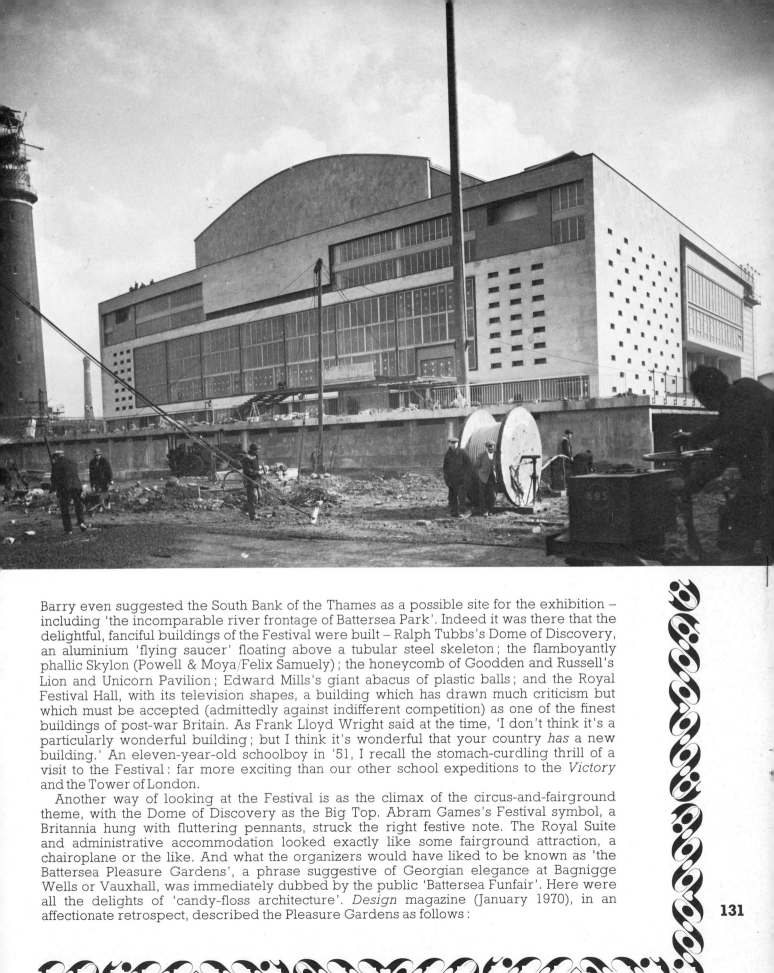

Barry even suggested the South Bank of the Thames as a possible site for the exhibition – including 'the incomparable river frontage of Battersea Park'. Indeed it was there that the delightful, fanciful buildings of the Festival were built – Ralph Tubbs's Dome of Discovery, an aluminium 'flying saucer' floating above a tubular steel skeleton; the flamboyantly phallic Skylon (Powell & Moya/Felix Samuely); the honeycomb of Goodden and Russell's Lion and Unicorn Pavilion; Edward Mills's giant abacus of plastic balls; and the Royal Festival Hall, with its television shapes, a building which has drawn much criticism but which must be accepted (admittedly against indifferent competition) as one of the finest buildings of post-war Britain. As Frank Lloyd Wright said at the time, 'I don't think it's a particularly wonderful building; but I think it's wonderful that your country *has* a new building.' An eleven-year-old schoolboy in '51, I recall the stomach-curdling thrill of a visit to the Festival: far more exciting than our other school expeditions to the *Victory* and the Tower of London.

Another way of looking at the Festival is as the climax of the circus-and-fairground theme, with the Dome of Discovery as the Big Top. Abram Games's Festival symbol, a Britannia hung with fluttering pennants, struck the right festive note. The Royal Suite and administrative accommodation looked exactly like some fairground attraction, a chairoplane or the like. And what the organizers would have liked to be known as 'the Battersea Pleasure Gardens', a phrase suggestive of Georgian elegance at Bagnigge Wells or Vauxhall, was immediately dubbed by the public 'Battersea Funfair'. Here were all the delights of 'candy-floss architecture'. *Design* magazine (January 1970), in an affectionate retrospect, described the Pleasure Gardens as follows:

Restaurant furniture, Royal Festival Hall, 1951. The chair had a
moulded plywood back and a rubber-cushioned seat; the dumb
waiter was in tubular metal, timber and aluminium

An entrance gate which might have been run up by Wyatt or Batty Langley, crowned
with odd little crenellations and twiddly bits, sits between two plasterboard tower-
follies. Beyond this preposterous piece of nonsense were the Vista arcades, the
Vista bars, the obelisks and the fountains – and a wickerwork Fern House which acted
as a back drop for firework displays.

It was traditional Beaux Arts pastiche – right for Battersea, wrong for the South
Bank site. Not that the amusement gardens were without the occasional flash of
whimsical inspiration. All kinds of English eccentricities kept popping up. A tree
walk, a tree restaurant worthy of something out of the Babar books, and Rowland
Emett's fantastically detailed Far Tottering to Oyster Creek railway. Those of us who
were mere schoolboys at the time still speak of the *Nellie, Neptune* and *Wild Goose*
with bated breath. How could anyone protest that the engines ran on standard Lister
diesels when they were garnished with tablespoon turbine blades and cylinders
made from rum barrels?

The Pleasure Gardens contained Gothic plasterboard follies designed by John Piper
and Osbert Lancaster; James Gardner's Lumascope; the calligraphic excesses of Patrick
Gwynne's Crescent Restaurant, like a pavilion for effeminate jousters; a 'gazebo' selling
Eldorado ice-cream, Lewitt-Him's Festival Clock of eccentric astrological design; and
Victorian street lamps as top-knots for kiosks selling Kia-Ora soft drinks.

Whatever may have been the worthier aims of the Festival organizers – to promote
exports, draw foreign tourists and 'bring both credit and profit to the capital of the Empire
while at the same time providing millions with enjoyment' (to quote from Gerald Barry's
original letter) – the main legacy it left, when the revels were ended, the baseless fabric
dissolved and the insubstantial pageant faded, was a rampant taste for eccentricity,
whimsy and Victoriana. The three seemed to go naturally together. It was natural for men
after the war to crave for the secure and spacious Victorian age, of which they were
reminded first by the centenary of the Great Exhibition in 1951 and then by the Coronation of 1953 which put a young queen on the throne of England for the first time since
Victoria. It was natural for men to react against a decade of regimentation, either in war or
austerity, in favour of the eccentric side of the Victorians. This reaction is seen in the
ballooning escapades of *Around the World in Eighty Days,* in the characters portrayed by

Alec Guinness in *Kind Hearts and Coronets,* in the balloons, penny-farthing bicycles and archaic wheel-chairs which became clichés of design and window-dressing. Edith Sitwell's book *The English Eccentrics* of 1933 was reissued in 1950 and 1958; and C. R. Hewitt contributed an article on 'Small Eccentrics' to *The Saturday Book* of 1951. Besides the chi-chi shops selling Victoriana, there was a growing serious interest in Victorian art and design: John Steegman's *Consort of Taste* was published in 1950, Nikolaus Pevsner's *High Victorian Design* in 1951; in 1953 Goodhart-Rendel's 1934 Slade Lectures on Victorian architecture were published for the first time; Henry Russell Hitchcock's *Early Victorian Architecture* appeared in 1954; T. S. R. Boase's paper on the decoration of the Houses of Parliament was read in 1954 and his Oxford volume on Victorian Art appeared in 1959; in 1958 the Victorian Society was founded. A study of the great Victorian portrait photographer Julia Margaret Cameron, by Helmut Gernsheim, was published as early as 1948. On its jacket it had trellis-work which was an easily recognizable Victorian motif, seen also in the latticed design of R. Y. Goodden's showcases for the printing section of the 'Enterprise Scotland' exhibition (Scottish Committee of the Council of Industrial Design, 1949); in openwork shoes by Joyce of California (1946); in many pavilions in the Festival of Britain; in the trellis gardens at Clifton; and, in Continental interpretations, in Domenico Mortellito's and Alex Thierry's absurd 'Corset' chairs (1941 and 1949 respectively) or the more ingenious and elegant trellis chairs by Guglielmo Ulrich (1948). Use of a trellis design could also be seen in a 1950 advertisement for the Oil Industry Information Committee of America by Lynd Ward, who in 1930 had designed that sinister 'novel in woodcuts' *God's Man*.[1] With the fashion for Victoriana, there may also have been a touch of the Red Queen's criss-cross snood in the taste for lattice-work. In clothes fashion of the forties, the lattice fashion is seen in the heavy veils of women's hats and in the use of tartans. In *Shocking Life* (1954), Elsa Schiaparelli wrote:

Lattice plus Victoriana; jacket design by Bainbridge for Helmut Gernsheim's *Julia Margaret Cameron*, 1948

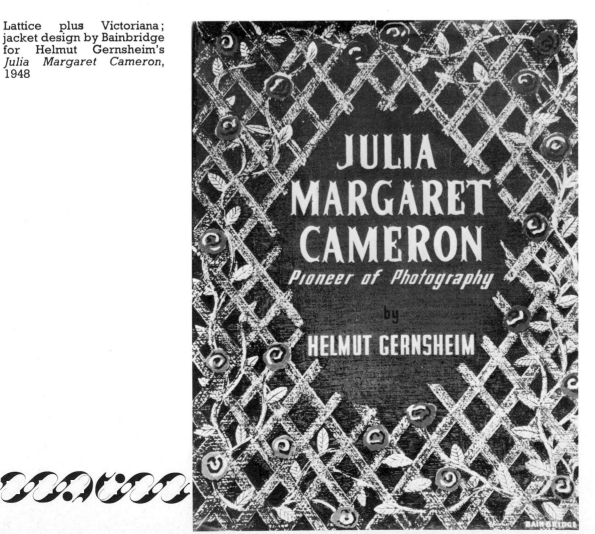

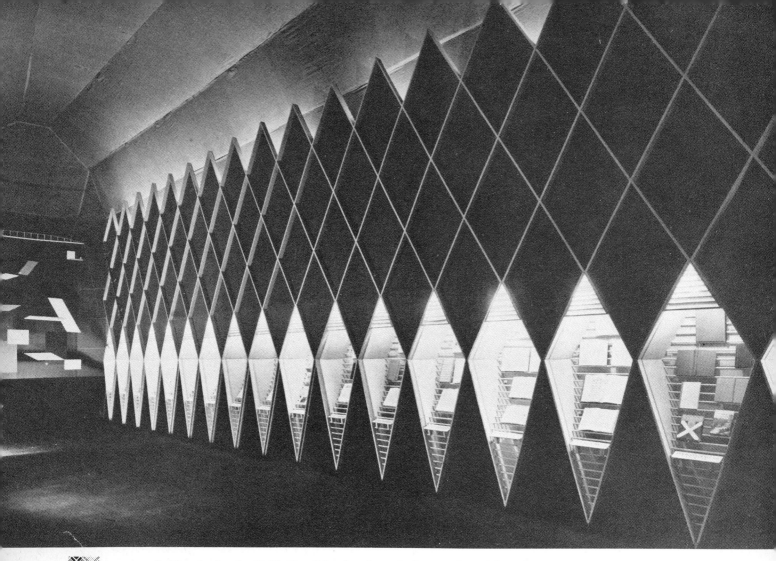

Lattice design by R. Y. Goodden for the printing section of the 'Enterprise Scotland' exhibition, Scottish Committee of the Council of Industrial Design, 1949

I became intensely interested in British textiles and visited all kinds of factories in England and Scotland. . . . We were spotted and driven to the house of Duncan MacLeod of Skenbow, where some of the most striking tweeds in existence are made. The whole family were 'out of this world' and delightful. They came down to dinner, thirty-two of them – even the children – wearing the most beautiful tartans, tartans of every colour, pink, blue, periwinkle and lettuce green; with topaz and amethyst buttons! . . . The men . . . in spite of their fanciful dress, were more virile than many city men who feel that to wear a spot of colour on their waistcoats might deprive them of their manhood. . . . Early in the morning the children, already splendid in their gay kilts, came into my room like puppies wanting to play. I spent the day at the mills choosing colours and patterns, full of admiration for the skill and the inherent, unerring taste of those who designed them. I was shown the different herbs and plants that give the dyes, dyes that are absolutely pure.

And in the epilogue to her book, she is discovered 'lying on an orange sofa made in Paris by Jean Franck of Moroccan leather, wrapped in a vivid Scotch rug of yellow and black tartan'.

Trellis-back chair by Guglielmo Ulrich, Italy, 1948

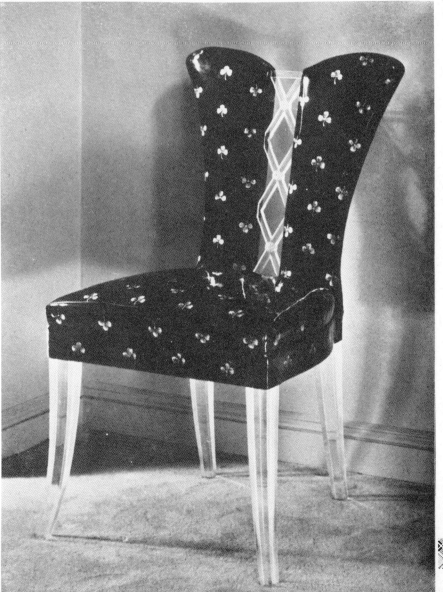

'Corset-back' chair in
perspex (plexiglas) and
black patent leather,
designed by Domenico
Mortellito

135

For Teenagers

Above
1950s use of trellis. Illustration
from *Party Pieces* by Julia
Clements

136

Tartan plus Victoriana: 'Girl in Crinoline'
by Louis Icart, New York

The taste for eccentricity is seen in the popularity of cartoonists such as Emett, who besides the Festival railway designed other amazing machines like the Featherstone-Kite Openwork Basket-weave Mk. 2 Gentleman's Flying Machine' (wickerwork again), Ronald Searle of the Lemon Hart Rum advertisements and the malevolently crazy St Trinian's School ('Hands up the girl who burnt down the East Wing last night'), and Gerard Hoffnung, who made a famous speech at the Oxford Union in the 1950s and who organized a concert for vacuum-cleaners at the Royal Festival Hall.[2] The Festival of Britain contained an 'Eccentrics' Corner', including a smoke-grinding machine, an egg round-about (circus again), a collapsible rubber bus, a tea set made of fish bones, and a 'device for keeping the nose out of the tea'. Michael Frayn has written: 'A certain melancholy British whimsy crept in elsewhere uninvited. The ministry of Pensions asked that room should be found for ''a modest display of artificial limbs''. A Midlands firm wondered if space could be found for some shrouds and coffin fittings. Another manufacturer sought permission to exhibit a model of the South Bank made out of toilet rolls.'

Whimsy

There was a growing interest during the late forties and the fifties in eccentric architecture of the past. Much was written on follies, including the mock ruins which John Piper painted with the laconic line of a puritannical British Dufy, setting them against wind-sweep and stormcloud. (The King, coming upon him in the grounds of Windsor one day, said, 'I'm sorry, Piper, it looks as if we're in for a fine day.') There was a revived taste for 'sharrawaggy' – the studied unconventionalism of Cathay; the word was even used by Sir Gerald Barry in describing the enthusiasm which had overtaken the Festival organizers: 'an irresistible mood of sharrawaggy and slightly unhinged romance'.[3] The Royal Pavilion, Brighton, which the Brighton Corporation had wanted to pull down in the 1930s, was restored to its Regency splendour by Dr Clifford Musgrave, and was purchased by the townspeople in 1951. Princess Elizabeth, who visited the Pavilion in that year, asked what had become of the original furniture. 'The only thing I could think of', Musgrave reports, 'was a line of Wordsworth: ''It lay about you in your infancy''.' Much of the original furniture was returned as a result of this conversation; Chinese landscapes began to appear from behind veils of varnish and municipal cigar smoke; and in 1952 the original silver-gilt of George IV was lent by the Crown. A new life began for the most exotic palace in Europe, the Karma Sutra of architecture. It represented, as Musgrave has said, 'Kubla Khan, Lallah Rookh, swooning sensuality, the earthly paradise of Hindustan, the crystallization of Shelley's ''Adamastor'' and ''Indian Serenade''.'

Frivolous arts flourished in the fifties, such as flower arranging and paper sculpture. Julia Clements's *Party Pieces,* a flower arrangement book written at the end of the fifties,[4] suggests that an 'amusing informal decoration' can be made 'by sticking Daisies, Chrysanthemums or any hard-stemmed flowers into a marrow. The marrow is surrounded by red

1950s art; flower arrangement, a *cul de lampe* from *Party Pieces* by Julia Clements

and green peppers and held firm by a large pin-holder.' Arthur Sadler's book on paper sculpture (1947) containing some delightful conceits, was reissued, 'completely revised' in 1951. Philip Halsman's *Jump Book* (Deutsch 1959) is another perfect example of fifties whimsy. This enterprising photographer went round persuading celebrities to jump in the air, including Judge Learned Hand (born 1872, 'America's most respected jurist'), Grace Kelly, the Duke and Duchess of Windsor, Clare Boothe Luce, Richard M. Nixon and Adlai E. Stevenson, Keith McHugh, President of the American Telephone Company, Aldous Huxley, John Steinbeck, Father d'Arcy, Walter Gropius and Marilyn Monroe. The *piece de resistance* of the book was Salvador Dali jumping: 'This portrait of Salvador Dali ("Dali Atomicus") was made during the artist's atomic period, in which he painted everything in suspension. It took 28 triple throws of cats and 28 splashes of water to obtain in the 28th exposure a composition which suited the author's demanding taste.' The only person who refused to jump to Halsman's bidding was Edith Sitwell, who told *The Sunday Times* 'This horrid little man came to see me. "Jump!" he said. "The Duchess of Windsor has jumped for me." "I don't care," I said. "*I'm* not jumping for you." ' One is reminded of the English businessman whose casual remark to a German visitor on a fine March day, 'Spring in the air', provoked an outraged 'Vy should I?'

Other examples of fifties whimsy are the 'Carrier-Pigeon' costume designed by Charles Montaigne and the costume of the future predicted by *Amazing Stories* magazine in 1952 (accurately enough, if one were to judge by Allen Jones's book *Waitress*, 1972, as both feature a bottomless dress). Also: sun-glasses in the form of revolvers joined muzzle to muzzle, or alarmingly flared and spangled; pearls taking the place of musical notes in an Italian fifties music sheet of Mendelssohn ('Perle Musicali'); plastic flowers in the transparent lid of a handbag, plastic dice in the transparent heels of a pair of high-heel shoes; a crinolined plastic woman as tape-measure container; a plastic high-heeled shoe as pin-cushion. The 'mobile' was another whimsical art-form at its height of popularity in the fifties. Edgar S. Bley's *Have Fun with your Son,* written in 1959, told one how to make mobiles from coat hangers, feathers and drinking straws.

1950s whimsy: Laurie Lee official caption writer of the Festival of Britain with the 'egg roundabout' in the Eccentrics' Corner of the Festival, 1951

1950s whimsy: plastic sunglasses in the form of revolvers joined muzzle to muzzle, Dougie Field, and extravagantly flared plastic sunglasses Let it Rock, James, Chelsea, London

1950s whimsy; the 'smoke-grinding machine' from the Eccentrics' Corner of the Festival of Britain

140

Left
1950s whimsy: the 'Carrier-Pigeon' look by Charles Montaigne, 1953 collection

1950s whimsy: coloured dice in the transparent plastic heels of a pair of high-heeled shoes. Michael and Gerlinde Costiff

1950s whimsy: iridescent plastic handbag with clear plastic handles and plastic flowers within clear plastic lid. Digby Howard

MENDELSSOHN

Sulle ali del canto

PER PIANOFORTE

Perle Musicali

CHIESA E
DEL MAGLIO

RICORDI

2/6

1950s whimsy: pearls as musical notes on a music-sheet cover

1950s whimsy: plastic pin-cushion in the form of a high-heeled shoe; and plastic tape-measure holder in the form of a woman in a crinoline

Plastic photograph frame, 1950s.
Nick Adams

1950s whimsy: clothes of the future, from *Amazing Stories* magazine, USA, 1952

Lamp with Negro motif, English, 1950s

144

Lamp in the form of a Negro head with turban, 1950s. Dougie Field

Radical changes in design style are usually detrimental to certain arts and beneficial to others. The geometric rigours of Art Deco were in general unsuited to the malleable clay of ceramics, but well suited to arts where bold rectilinear stylization and mass-production were essential, such as posters and book jackets. In the same way, fifties whimsy, while it was only appropriate in architecture of festivals or coronations, where light-hearted bravura was expected, and led to furniture and fittings which were interior 'follies', gave a much-needed fillip to the art of window display. Flippancy, showiness and shock were appropriate to an art ephemeral by nature, in which surface was all and where, once the eye had been caught, there was no thought of moving passions or of appealing to a profound understanding. Two books of the time give a good idea of the developments: *Window Display,* a large book of 1951 edited by Walter Herdeg, in which experts from different countries gave an account of what was happening in window design in France, Great Britain, Italy, Switzerland, the United States, and other countries; and the smaller but admirable *Window Display* by Natasha Kroll (1954). Together the books form a comprehensive compendium of design motifs of the period – musical instruments (cf. Hoffnung), heraldry, balloons, trellis, disembodied hands, birdcages, fishing nets, lobster pots, umbrellas and so on. Victoriana was in, as John A. Rosenberg, the New York contributor to the 1951 book, specifically says. In particular, there was a fascination with old machines. The most popular was the penny-farthing bicycle, which figures both as a drawing in Natasha Kroll's book, and in two designs in different countries photographed for the 1951 Herdeg book: Artina, Paris, dress fabrics (designer, Jeanne Dubois-Dugrenet) and Saks Fifth Avenue, Beverly Hills (designer, Jim Buckley). But also old typewriters, scales, 'old crock' motor cars (cf. the film *Genevieve* made in 1953, and the jacket of E. W. Borjeson's book *Fartens herre eller slav . . . ,* Stockholm 1949) and cranky old locomotives like those designed by Emett for the Festival Pleasure Gardens, or that delightfully drawn by Philip Gough on the cover of *Love on a Branch Line* (1959) by John Hadfield, then and still editor of *The Saturday Book.* The publisher's blurb to this book said:

> The 'Branch Line' is an Emett-like affair which transports the reader from the silly realities of our present world to the much more sensible and immensely more enjoyable depths of an almost mythical East Anglia, where a backwoodsman peer lives in a private railway train, playing vintage jazz as an accompaniment to the amorous dalliance of three gorgeously amoral daughters. . . .

Paris

Another set of fifties motifs, immensely popular among designers, and not just in window display, derived from the opening up of Paris again to tourists. In the war Paris had of course been occupied. After the war most English people were too hard-up to go there, but with the gradually increasing affluence of the fifties, the English again crossed the Channel to brave the frogs' legs, garlic breath and pissoirs. Symbolically, if somewhat prematurely, the Golden Gallery Press, London, reissued in 1948 George Augustus Sala's enjoyably bombastic book *Paris Herself Again,* originally published in 1880 as a collection of his despatches in *The Daily Telegraph* of 1878–9, after the Franco–Prussian War. Beverley Nichols contributed to *Leader* magazine of 27 May 1950 an article entitled 'First Time in Paris'. Like Sala, the English of the fifties were interested in the delights of Gay Paree. 'I love Paris in the springtime', a fifties pop song ran; and another began

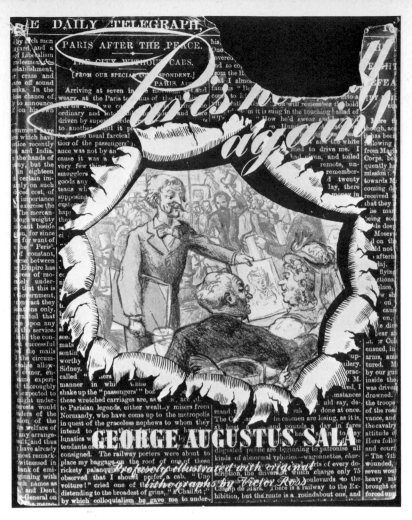

Jacket of the 1948 reissue by the Golden Gallery Press, London, of G. A. Sala's *Paris Herself Again*

How would you like to be
Down by the Seine with me ?
Under the bridges of Paris with you,
I'd make your dreams come true.

Victor Young and his Singing Strings recorded a series of 45 r.p.m. records for Decca called 'April in Paris' (1949) and the Boston Pops Orchestra made a similar set called 'Gaité (*sic*) Parisienne'. H. E. Bates sent his Larkin family over to France in *A Breath of French Air* (Michael Joseph 1959). The publisher's blurb captures the ooh-la-la adventure of it all :

> In *A Breath of French Air*, Pop Larkin and his handsome family of seven (all born without benefit of clergy) step outside their rural paradise for an excursion into another world. Armed with plenty of tax-free cash, their Rolls-Royce and little French, they take their first holiday abroad. Their intensely English but wholly unconventional reactions to life in France, especially its ideas on love and food, are in that same vein of slightly Rabelaisian picaresque slapstick that delighted readers of *The Darling Buds of May* on both sides of the Atlantic. . . .

China plates were decorated with Lautrecian café scenes and poodles. In the 1957 film *Will Success Spoil Rock Hunter*? Jayne Mansfield wore outfits identical to those of her poodle, and they took baths together ; an even more titillating bathtub scene was a number by Jane Russell in the archetypally fifties musical *The French Line* (1953). Eiffel Towers were printed on headscarfs. José Ferrer stumped about valiantly on his knees as Lautrec in the film *Moulin Rouge* (1953).

Pottery plates of the early 1950's decorated with 'Parisian' motifs

Headscarf decorated with Parisian motifs. Vernon Lambert

Paris Follies of 1956, poster for
film directed by Leslie Goodwins

Front and back views of
'Paris head' in plaster, *c.*
1956

PARIS HEAD

The artist, who so lately had only been acceptable if he 'did his bit' for the war effort and painted camouflage, was now free again – encouraged – to go Bohemian; the late forties and early fifties were the heyday of artists' Soho and 'beatniks'. The artist's palette is one of the most frequently encountered motifs of the fifties, whether in ashtrays, film posters, brooches, vases, advertisements, calendars, table shapes or science-fiction designs by the brilliant Virgil Finlay. The Earl Epps Smoke House (since destroyed), at San Antonio, Texas was almost entirely composed of palette motifs, from table shapes to wall decoration.

148

Left
Palette brooch and 'corset' brooch, 1950s. Anton and Susan Marsh

Jacket design by James Fitton, for Stanley Jackson's *An Indiscreet Guide to Soho*

Porcelain model of girl's torso against palette-shaped background. Mark in underglaze blue 'by W. Goebel'. Incised 'Nasha 1956'. $14 \times 10 \times 3$ cm ($5\frac{1}{2} \times 4 \times 1\frac{1}{4}$ in.)

149

'Palette-able', one of a series of pin-ups by Elvgren, USA

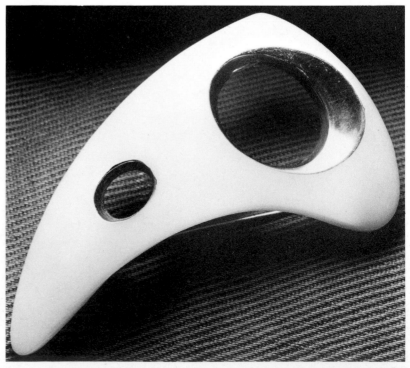

Pottery plate from 'Homemaker' set, 1950s, by Ridgway Pottery, Staffordshire

Right
Truncated palette brooch in plastic. Digby Howard

Palette-shaped calendar

Science and science fiction

In science proper the growing possibilities of space travel offered exciting new themes to be translated into the vocabulary of design. The marvels of early astronomy had inspired exquisite astronomical/astrological clocks, 'the clockwork of the heavens', beautiful toys of science like the fourteenth-century 'wheels within wheels' clock of Giovanni de Dondi of Padua which can be thought of as metallic architecture or in the terms of modern sculpture. In the rococo period of eighteenth-century Europe, scientific developments could be given a frivolous rococo interpretation. As a recent book on the period rather extravagantly puts it, 'the wonders revealed by the microscope were . . . merely a delight for the eye, and the thrilling phenomena of electricity a drawing-room diversion'.[5] Descartes' ponderous theory of vortices had been demolished by Isaac Newton. 'A Circumstance which has always appear'd wonderful to me,' wrote Voltaire, 'is, that such sublime Discoveries should have been made with the sole Assistance of a Quadrant and a little Arithmetic'.[6] It was even more diverting to reflect that the inspiration of the theory had been a falling apple; nothing was less grave, it seems, than gravity.

In the same way, space travel lent itself to fifties whimsy. It could be made the excuse for any kind of fantasy, just as the still unexplored parts of the earth had been to late nineteenth-century writers such as Conan Doyle. Science was catching up with science fiction. The French magazine *V* issued a space number ('L'Amour Sidéral') on 26 January 1947, with a centre spread on 'Les Voyageurs pour la Lune' and a back page of naughty cartoons: monsters from Mars ogle Parisian models; a man is finding it hard to keep his girlfriend in bed because of weightlessness; indicating a spacewoman with four breasts, one happy astronaut tells another that 'she'll be marvellous in 3-D movies'; a mincing homosexual says from his airship at the Venus stratogare 'I'd rather die than disembark on this planet infested with women'; and in an upstairs room a tin Lizzie tells her boyfriend, 'I can't undress because I'm an all-aluminium robot woman'. In America these were happy days for Superman and Captain Marvel; and in England in 1951 the Rev. Marcus Morris founded *Eagle* comic with its superbly drawn Dan Dare serial. His daughter Sally is still

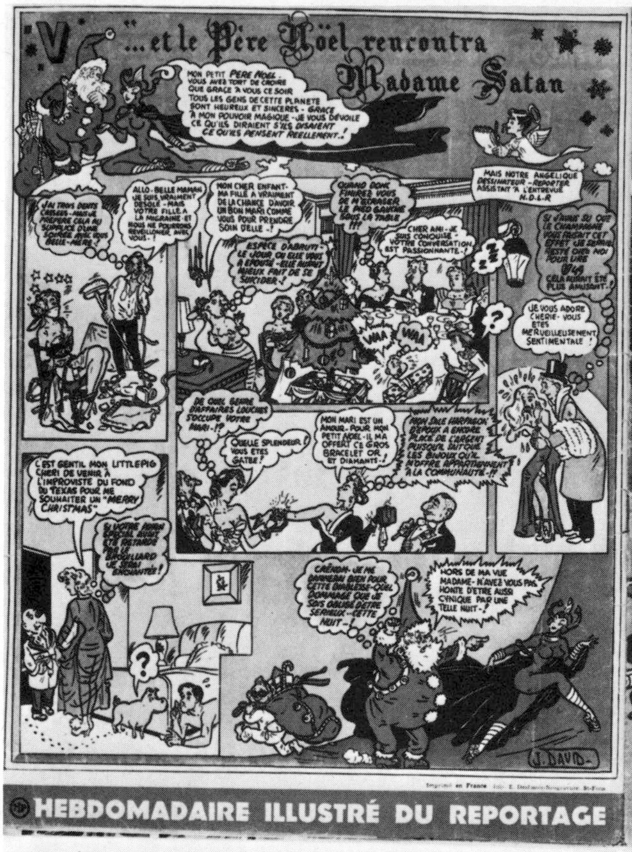

HEBDOMADAIRE ILLUSTRÉ DU REPORTAGE

NUMERO SPECIAL
NOËL

35 frs

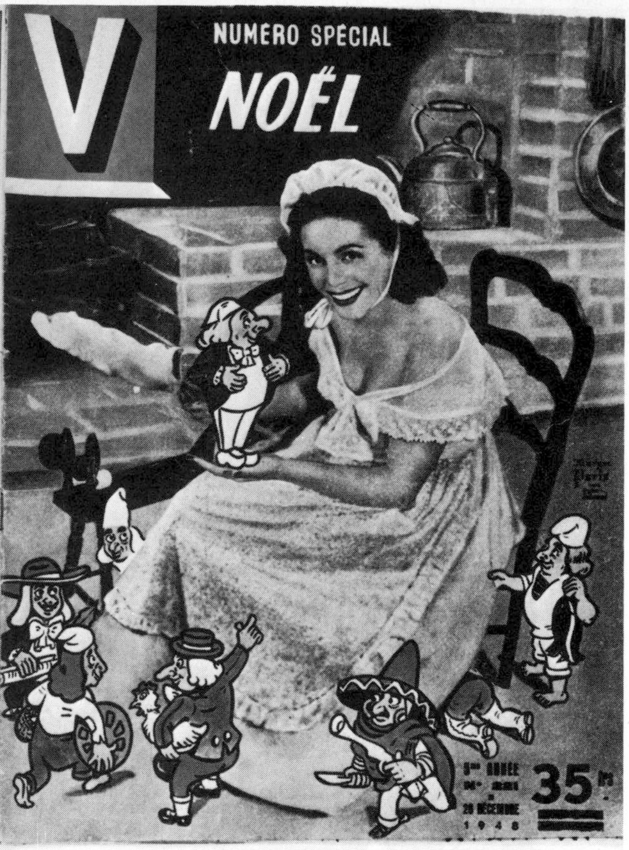

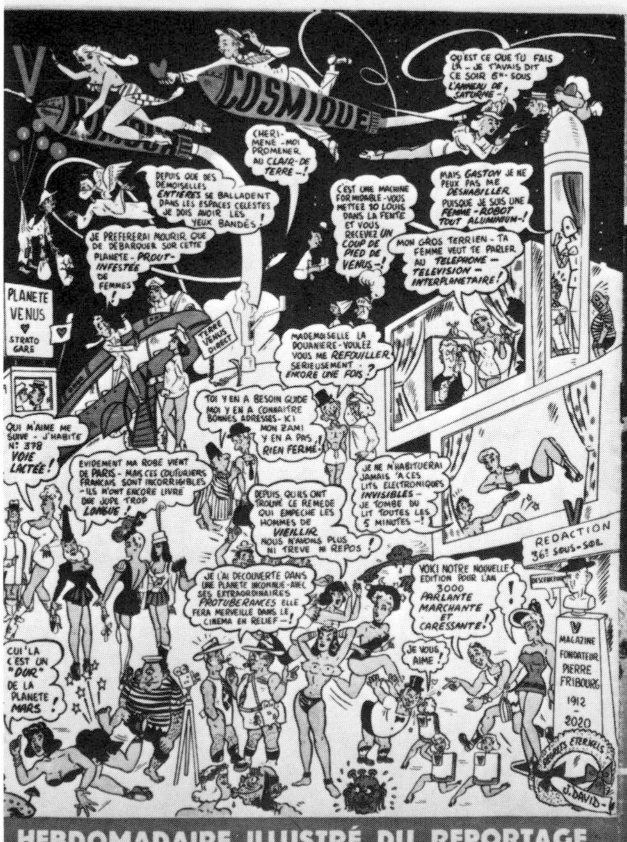

HEBDOMADAIRE ILLUSTRÉ DU REPORTAGE

L'AMOUR SIDÉRAL

12 frs
TOUTES LES SEMAINES

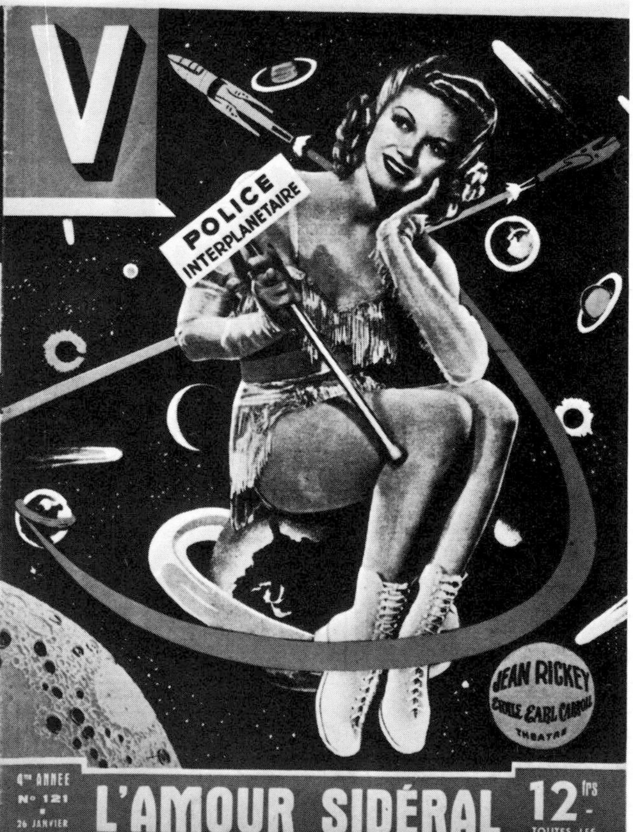

152

known as 'the Mekon' because, when she was a baby, her bald head was the model for that of the little green monster on an aerial motor-scooter who led the inscrutable green men, the Treens. The Space Age began on 4 October 1957, with the ascent of Sputnik I, the Russian artificial satellite which circled the world sending out 'Bleep Bleep' signals picked up by new technology in every country. Sputniks, spinning planets and shooting stars became popular motifs on crockery.

The most potent image from outer space was the flying saucer. The phrase was first used on 24 June 1947. On that day Kenneth Arnold took off from Chehalis, Washington, in an aeroplane specially designed for mountain work. He was on a mercy mission to look for a lost C-46 Marine transport plane that had crashed somewhere in the Cascade Mountains. Visibility was good, and suddenly Arnold saw two bright flashes and a formation of nine gleaming objects coming from the direction of Mount Baker. They were flying close to the peaks at what seemed to be a vast speed. As the formation flew on towards Mount Rainier, Arnold was in a good position to triangulate the speed between the peaks of Mount Rainier and Mount Adams, and found they were going at 1,200 m.p.h. He later described their motion to reporters as being like 'saucers skimming over water'. The press headlined them as 'Flying Saucers' and the name stuck. A series of sightings of Unidentified Flying Objects followed; the major ones are listed by Brinsley Le Poer Trench in *The Flying Saucer Story* (1966). Le Poer Trench has an ingenious explanation for the intensified interest in the Earth by flying saucer drivers in the late forties and fifties:

The reasons why they have not landed openly, we believe, are due mainly to the fact that their intentions most surely would be misunderstood, even more than they are already. Secondly, it is due to our tardy sociological and technological development. For several thousand years, just in the field of technology alone, we had nothing at all to speak of, and compared to them were a very unenlightened and primitive people preoccupied with plundering and ravaging our planet as well as ourselves.... Then, in 1945, we exploded the atom bomb. Once we had unlocked the secrets of nuclear fission they knew we were on our way. Space travel would soon follow. Since that time the earth has elicited much interest and has been under constant surveillance by our space neighbours.

Heaters in the form of a flying saucer. English, 1950s

Left
Covers of the French magazine V for 20 December 1948 (top) and 26 January 1947

FLYING SAUCERS

By ALLEN GLASSER

From deepest Space the disks appear,

Like visitants from There to Here.

Yet no man knows from what strange world,

In realms remote, these disks were hurled,

Nor what their mission here may be—

Galactic friend or enemy?

Supposing, then, these Saucers came

As viewers of the deadly game

Unfolding on our sorry sphere,

Concerned with war and hate and fear.

Enclosed within, the Watchers wait

Release when Man has met his fate—

Successors, they, to Earth's estate!

From *Wonder Story Annual*

The interest in flying saucers during the fifties is illustrated by the publication of many books and articles.[7] The flying saucer motif spread through widely differing qualities of art, from cheap electric fires to silver trophy cups designed by Porteous Wood for Asprey's. A new sweet called 'flying saucers' was made in the fifties, consisting of round rice-paper bubbles containing sherbet. And I remember a comic in which a story about a boy learning to fly one of these machines was titled 'The Saucerer's Apprentice'.

Illustration to 'Doomstruck', a story by Clyde B. Smith in *Fantastic Stories*, USA 1953

When the planetoid struck, the world would end. . . .

Pottery bowl in the form of a ship, marked 'Wade, England, "Shooting Star"'. 1950s

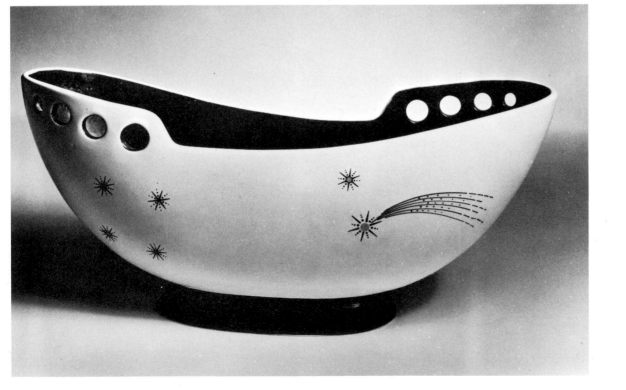

House designed by Martial E Scull, USA *c.* 1946 designed to withstand atomic bomb raids. Built of thick concrete and lead and surrounded by an anti-blast wall, it was fitted with an automatic device to seal all windows, doors and ventilators. The device would be triggered by an 'electric eye' on the flagpole responding to the flash from an atomic bomb

But the trick of design which gave the fifties their most characteristic look, and which most immediately evokes the period today, is the bobbles on sticks, or joined together by struts, which fifties designers, in their whimsical way, called the 'cocktail cherry' style. We see it, early on, in Graham Sutherland's title-page to David Gascoyne's *Poems, 1937-1942* (Editions Poetry, London 1943) ; in the feet of chairs and tables and a revolving nudes lamp made in St Paul, Minnesota ; in the decoration of popular television ornaments containing mirrors and real butterflies ; in Edward Mills's so-called 'abacus' at the Festival of Britain ; and in many wallpaper and textile patterns, including that designed by W. Hertzberger for Turnbull and Stockdale in 1956.

At the Cavendish laboratory, Cambridge, England, in 1946 : a model of 'the architecture of matter'

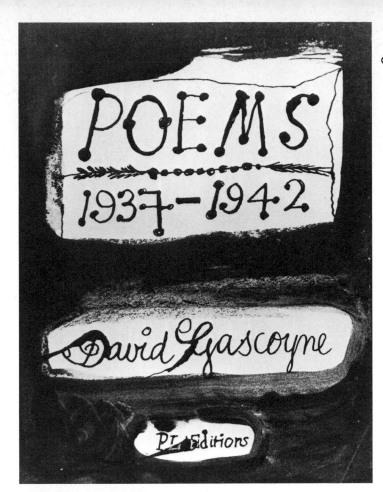

Title-page designed by Graham Sutherland for *Poems 1937-1942* by David Gascoyne, 1943

Below
Revolving 'nudie' lamp with 'cocktail-cherry' legs, made in St Paul, Minnesota, USA 1950s

Two eye-shaped television-top ornaments containing mounted butterflies and mirror, and with 'molecular structure' motifs. Dougie Field.

157

Edward Mills's 'Abacus' screen to Waterloo Road; Festival of Britain. 1951

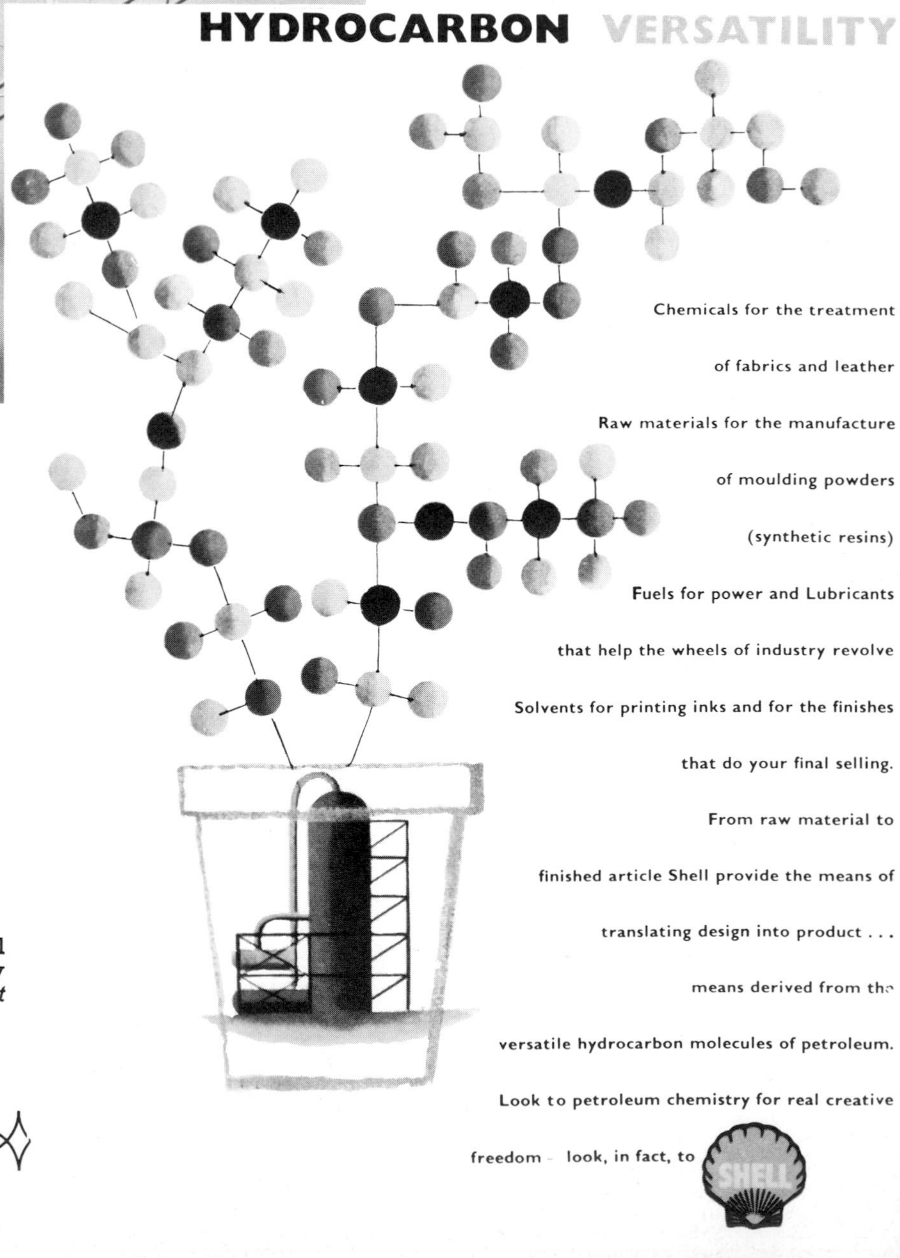

Advertisement for Shell Chemicals, designed by F. H. K. Henrion. *Contact* 1948

HYDROCARBON VERSATILITY

Chemicals for the treatment

of fabrics and leather

Raw materials for the manufacture

of moulding powders

(synthetic resins)

Fuels for power and Lubricants

that help the wheels of industry revolve

Solvents for printing inks and for the finishes

that do your final selling.

From raw material to

finished article Shell provide the means of

translating design into product . . .

means derived from the

versatile hydrocarbon molecules of petroleum.

Look to petroleum chemistry for real creative

freedom — look, in fact, to SHELL

The term 'cocktail cherry' is nicely descriptive, but it gives no clue as to the reason for the new style. Possibly it derived in part from all those wartime charts 'putting people in the picture' which showed how everyone's function in the war effort joined up with everyone else's by the use of blobs and linking straight lines. However, far more, I believe, it derived from nuclear physics, with its breaking-down of matter into atoms and molecules, often imaged by 'cocktail cherry' type models. The most terrible image in the minds of men of the fifties was the explosion of the Atomic Bomb at Hiroshima in 1945, but atoms and molecules were also associated with the idea of building up, 'recon-struction', 'regeneration', as well as of breaking-down and destruction. This is suggested by Dorothy Wellesley's 1942 poem 'Lost Planet', embodying so many Austerity/Binge images and ideas:

Now in purest graduation
Like light through lattices – through slats
That clipt together and would not open
To the light the light of adoration:

The light is a portent – it is potent
Of much we guessed at in dark time,
Darker darker – than this time this time
Now importunate, impotent
Devoid of all but flux
Devoid of all but plasm
Flux, plasm, devoid of fusion
Capable only of light or dark
In this breaking down, this utter orgasm
Explosion on explosion.

For now – in this cataclysm
Of War of War – the storm has torn the atom
And shattered and shattered – the electron
Which must formulate formulate – again
There is no more pain no pain – only gain.
We shall be saved by the agony
By the pain,
And behold by this the vision
Of the formulation of the shattered matter
Of our bodies, and of our souls
Our souls which were matter,
Our souls second-best only to our bodies. . . .

After the Deluge the unknown formulation. . . .[8]

It was no accident that Dali wanted to be shown in the *Jump Book* as 'Dali Atomicus'; it was as much the artist's assimilation of one kind of scientific advance as Gerard Hoffnung's gramophone records, 'The Hoffnung Interplanetary Festival' and 'The Hoffnung Astro-nautical Festival', were of another. *Photo World* of July 1946 had included an article by T. P. Gallagher, 'Gateway to the Atomic Future', about the Cavendish Laboratory in Cambridge, England, including a photograph of a model which demonstrated 'the architecture of matter. Balls are atoms. An orange magnified to the size of the earth would show atoms this large.' Gallagher wrote of the artificial transmutation of the elements achieved by Cockcroft and Walton as of a new philosopher's stone.

The other instrument for 'torturing the atom' is the cyclotron, worth about £100,000. This massive drum-like machine converts a few hundred volts to the equivalent in accelerating power of five to twenty million. Sub-atomic charged particles, protons, deuterons (nuclei of heavy hydrogen or nuclei of helium), are picked up from the centre of the cyclotron and whirled round and round in an ever widening spiral path under the action of powerful electric and magnetic fields. Finally a beam of particles is shot out through a window in the rim of the cyclotron on to the target whose nuclei are torn apart.

The best-known example of an atomic model translated into art is the Brussels Atomium, a cocktail-cherry building which is represented on certain Belgian banknotes today. A caption to one of the illustrations in E. D. S. Bradford's *Contemporary Jewellery and Silver Design* (1950) makes the derivation explicit:

> The analysis of atomic structure provides an unusual contemporary motif for this outstanding brooch by Roy C. King, which is constructed in gold and platinum, set with rubies and diamonds.

The cocktail-cherry style marks the reception into popular decorative art of a practice common in 'mainstream' canvas art for fifty or more years before: the bodying into visual images of new scientific concepts. In his recent book *The Ascent of Man* Dr Bronowski traces the revelations of atomic physics from the 'turning-point' in 1897 (J. J. Thomson's discovery of the electron), through the contributions of Rutherford, Bohr, Mosley, Chadwick, Enrico Fermi, Hans Bethe to the proof of the evolution of matter 'finally sealed in what I suppose to be the definitive analysis in 1957'. He has a brilliant passage on this transmutation of science into art:

1950s furnishing fabrics, including chair covering with 'molecular structure' motifs. Dougie Field

Ball clock (1949) designed for Herman Miller by George Nelson & Company, New York

This [Thomson's discovery of the electron] is the intellectual breakthrough with which modern physics begins. Here the great age opens. Physics becomes in those years the greatest collective work of science – no, more than that, the great collective work of art of the twentieth century.

I say 'work of art' because the notion that there is an underlying structure, a world within world of the atom, captured the imagination of artists at once. Art from the year 1900 on is different from the art before it, as can be seen in any original painter of the time: Umberto Boccioni, for instance, in *The Forces of a Street* or his *Dynamism of a Cyclist*. Modern art begins at the same time as modern physics because it begins in the same ideas.[9]

'Marshmallow' sofa (1956) designed for Herman Miller by George Nelson & Company, New York

Eye-shaped television-top ornament containing mounted butterfly, and with 'molecular' structure motif. Dougie Field.

He follows this idea through the juxtaposition of 'atoms' of colour by Seurat; the invention of X-ray pictures by Röntgen which caused artists to 'look for the bone beneath the skin', as in the structural analysis of Juan Gris; the inspiration the cubists took from families of crystals; and the search for hidden structure by the painters of Northern Europe such as Franz Marc and Jean Metzinger, 'a favourite with scientists'. Metzinger's *Woman on a Horse* was owned by Niels Bohr, who himself had achieved in 1913 that most artistic of concepts in physics, of 'opening a stained-glass window' into the atom by interpreting its colour spectrum. In this context, the 'cocktail cherry' style may seem a trivial and over-literal artistic interpretation of scientific developments. But it was a popular art form, which certainly affected people more (and affected more people) than the canvases of Jean Metzinger or even Picasso. While the popular decorative art form of the twenties and thirties, Art Deco, fed on art itself, and produced more or less colourable pastiches of cubism, the 'cocktail cherry' style was the first popular decorative art form to draw directly on science.

Another scientific development which had a strong effect on the decorative arts and architecture was the rapidly improving television set, which was replacing the fireplace as the focal point of the main living room. From the 'futuristic' contraption with midget screen shown at the Ideal Home Exhibition, London, of 1947, and sets that skulked inside imitation walnut cocktail cabinets, the television set passed through the more open but still small-screen example shown on the cover of the *Television Annual* for 1952 to the unabashed wide-screen set on cocktail-cherry legs, not needing to masquerade as anything else.[10] Straight copies of TV sets appeared in design, as in the digital electric clock patented by the Pennwood Numechron Co. of Pittsburgh, Pennsylvania, in 1955.

Digital electric clock, USA 1955.
14 × 9 × 9 cm (5½ × 3 × 3½ in.)

Television at the Ideal Home
Exhibition, London 1947

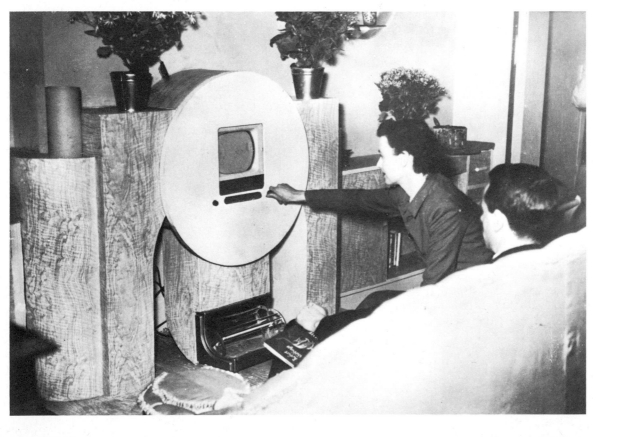

Cover of *The Television Annual* for 1952

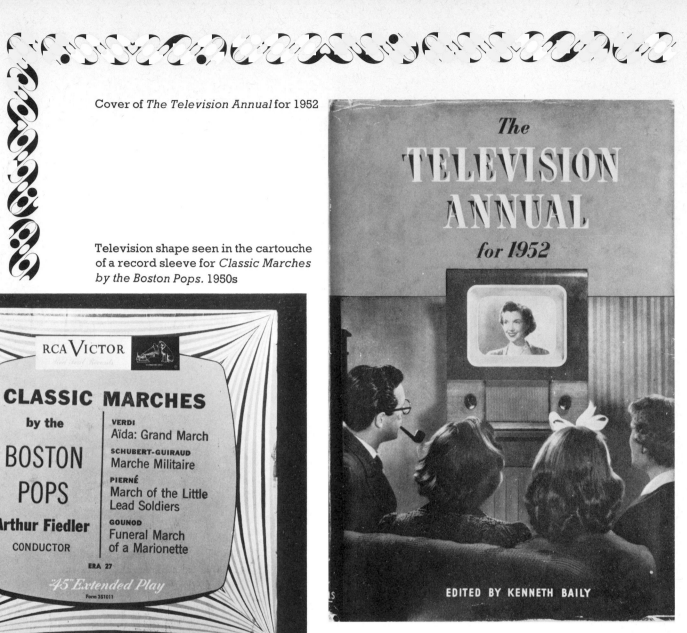

The
TELEVISION ANNUAL
for 1952

EDITED BY KENNETH BAILY

Television shape seen in the cartouche of a record sleeve for *Classic Marches by the Boston Pops.* 1950s

RCA VICTOR

CLASSIC MARCHES
by the

BOSTON

POPS

Arthur Fiedler
CONDUCTOR

ERA 27

45" Extended Play
Form 351011

VERDI
Aïda: Grand March

SCHUBERT-GUIRAUD
Marche Militaire

PIERNÉ
March of the Little Lead Soldiers

GOUNOD
Funeral March of a Marionette

Mace designed by Gerald Benney for Leicester University in 1957, with television-shape head. The Worshipful Company of Goldsmiths

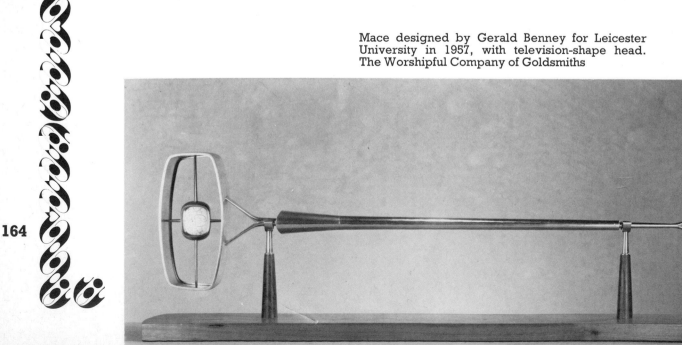

But the shape of the television screen, with its arc sides, also entered design less directly, as in the sleeve of the Boston Pops 'Classic Marches' record, various elevations of the Royal Festival Hall, the head of the mace Gerald Benney designed for Leicester University in 1957, and the windows of Chestergate House, Vauxhall Bridge Road, London, the best example I know of a thoroughgoing High Fifties building (designed by Sir John Burnet, Tait & Partners, in the late fifties, but not occupied as offices until the early sixties). Unlike the cocktail-cherry fashion, the TV screen shape has lingered in design (television, after all, has lingered in social life). A good example is the new 50p piece in England, with its arc sides.

The Coronation

The first grand-scale use of television was at the Coronation of 1953. Through the medium, at least 25,000,000 people in Britain watched the ceremony, and they were joined by viewers in France, Holland, Denmark and North-West Germany. Except for two short breaks, there were seven hours of continuous television broadcasting.[11] Many people who had watched the great occasion on neighbours' sets now ordered their own. In 1958 several additional transmitters were opened, bringing BBC television to virtually the whole population of Great Britain and Northern Ireland.

The Coronation was a chance to apply all the tricks of pomp and show and visual badinage learnt at the Festival of Britain, and the Minister of Works, Lord Eccles, wisely asked the Festival team led by Hugh Casson to join his own design staff under Eric Bedford to stage-manage the event. The obvious theme in everyone's mind was that a Queen Elizabeth was coming to the throne again. The first one had been a Good Thing, with armadas scattered, Spanish gold seized, empire extended, and a mellow cultural stability established in which a Shakespeare or Hilliard could flourish. The prime ornament of the Coronation, Eric Bedford's showy Mall arches, rammed the theme home: the princess's crowns suspended from parabolic steel arches were made up of calligraphic figures-of-eight like the flourish under Elizabeth I's signature (though the crowns were joined to the arches by a 'cocktail-cherry' network very like Edward Mills's Festival abacus). James Gardner turned Kensington Gore into a jousting arena. Misha Black medievalized the buildings of St James's. Plymouth staged a pageant on the Hoe, including the inevitable re-enactment of Drake's insouciant game of bowls. Bristol re-launched John Cabot down the Avon at Sandwich, Kent. Good Queen Bess offered sanctuary to French and Dutch refugees. Manchester Art Gallery held an exhibition of early Elizabethans. Liverpool held archery competitions, and 'all across the hills and downs of Britain, two thousand beacons blazed a chain of greetings, glowing where flames had once signalled the coming of the Spanish Armada'.[12] *The Young Elizabethan* magazine sold well, with its lively covers and illustrations by Sir John Verney. This was the peak of the fashion for heraldry, especially in Coronation souvenirs, which included a lion-and-unicorn mug well designed for Wedgwood by Richard Guyatt and even a handbag, designed for Metrolite by Henry Tydor, with the royal arms above the clasp. Whimsy was also allowed its place, in light bulbs of which the filament formed the letters 'E.R.' and pop-up children's books.

The 1951 Festival and the Coronation were the last flowering of the old establishment culture in Britain. The people were given what the Government and the Government's chosen agents wanted them to have, not what Billy Butlin or Val Parnell would have given them. The festivities were 'off the ration'; but they were Design Council approved – all Heal let loose, as someone remarked. Michael Frayn has put it well:

Electric light bulb Coronation souvenir, 1953

Cover of pop-up Coronation souvenir book, London, 1953

LONG LIVE THE QUEEN!

THE CORONATION BOOK
WITH REALISTIC POP-UP PICTURES

166

Festival Britain was the Britain of the radical middle-classes – the do-gooders; the readers of the *News Chronicle*, the *Guardian*, and the *Observer*; the signers of petitions; the backbone of the BBC. In short, the Herbivores, or gentle ruminants, who look out from the lush pastures which are their natural station in life with eyes full of sorrow for less fortunate creatures, guiltily conscious of their advantages, though not usually ceasing to eat the grass. . . . For a decade, sanctioned by the exigencies of war and its aftermath, the Herbivores had dominated the scene. By 1951 the regime which supported them was exhausted, and the Carnivores were ready to take over. The Festival was the last, and virtually the posthumous, work of the Herbivore Britain of the BBC News, the Crown Film Unit, the sweet ration, the Ealing comedies, Uncle Mac, Sylvia Peters . . . all the great fixed stars by which my childhood was navigated.[13] (Frayn was born in 1933.)

Frayn also singles out for quiet ridicule Gerald Barry's remark on the Festival: 'We envisage this as the people's show, not organized arbitrarily for them to enjoy, but put on largely by them, by us all, as an expression of a way of life in which we believe.' Frayn comments: 'It is the true voice of the forties speaking; not even the most Herbivorous of men, in our age of more highly sophisticated class consciousness and guilt, could stand up in public and announce that a committee consisting of a former newspaper editor, two senior civil servants, an architect, a theatre manager, a cinéaste, a palaeontologist, a public relations officer, and Huw Wheldon, was the People.'

But who were the Carnivores who were about to take over? What Frayn means by the term is a class more upper and aggressive than the Herbivores – 'the readers of the *Daily Express*; the Evelyn Waughs,[14] the cast of the Directory of Directors – the members of the upper- and middle-classes who believe that if God had not wished them to prey on all smaller and weaker creatures without scruple, he would not have made them as they are'. Frayn is right to the extent to which he is thinking in political terms, for it was in 1951, the year of the Festival, that a revitalized Tory party swept back to power under Winston Churchill after six years of Labour rule. But in social terms he was not right: for his Herbivores and Carnivores came from the same schools and belonged to the same clubs, and readers of the *News Chronicle* were not so very different from readers of the *Daily Express.* At any event, they were all middle-class or above. The real Carnivores rearing up in the fifties were the working-class teenagers, taking their wild, anti-social rock culture from America. Oscar Wilde as a young man had created the Aesthetic Movement and preached its gospel in America; but Wilde was the son of a titled Irish gentleman, an Oxford scholar who had run the gauntlet of establishment culture before rebelling against it. For the first time, in the 1950s, working-class youth with no scholastic polish was calling the tune, or rather shouting it. By the 1960s, when those teenagers were in their twenties, they had become part of the establishment culture. 'They' had taken over from 'Us' (or 'We' from 'Them', according to which side you were on).

Rock Culture

After the anodyne crooning of the forties, the lusty crowing animism of rock 'n' roll: the savage white smile of Little Richard, then dressed in baggy suits, not the mirror-sewn skintights he sports today; the choreographic panache of Bo Diddley; the commanding sexuality of Chuck Berry; the charismatic flabbiness of Chubby Checker; the puffy glamourlessness of Bill Haley which the famous greasy kiss-curl did nothing to mitigate. Over all, the godlike figure of Presley, with his sidekicks and imitators. In his poem 'Elvis Presley' (1957), Thom Gunn wrote:

> Two minutes long it pitches through some bar:
> Unreeling from a corner box, the sigh
> Of this one, in his gangling finery
> And crawling sideburns, wielding a guitar.
>
> The limitations where he found success
> Are ground on which he, panting, stretches out
> In turn, promiscuously by every note.
> Our idiosyncrasy and our likeness.
>
> We keep ourselves in touch with a mere dime:
> Distorting hackneyed words in hackneyed songs
> He turns revolt into a style, prolongs
> The impulse to a habit of the time.[15]

A typical English singer of the pre-rock fifties was the ample Alma Cogan, who wore hoop skirts like bell-tents and sang songs like 'You, Me and Us' ('We are my fa-vour-ite people'), 'The Naughty Lady of Shady Lane' ('She's got the town in a whirl'), and 'I Can't tell a Waltz from a Tango'. (A TV comedian told a joke about a street-barrow grocer called Shultz who got run over by a lorry, the punch-line being 'You couldn't tell a Shultz from a Mango'.) She was succeeded, and so were 'Give Me the Moonlight' (1955), 'Stranger in Paradise' (1955) and all the chirruping about Paris in the springtime, by 'Rock Around the Clock' (1955), 'Singing the Blues' (1957), Cliff Richard, Tommy Steele, and Adam Faith, ordinary lads like you and me who suddenly found themselves earning

Music sheet, 'Prettier Than You', English, 1950s

Opposite
Juke-box, the 'Chantal Meteor 200' designed by David Fry, 1952. This piece fetched £360 at Sotheby's, Belgravia, in 1973. Height 150 cm (59 in.). Sotheby's Belgravia

168

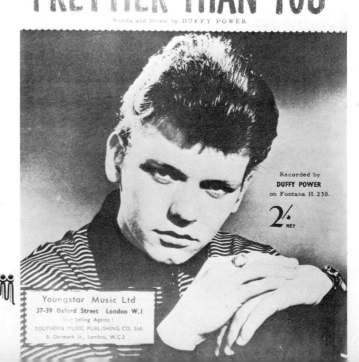

PRETTIER THAN YOU

Words and Music by DUFFY POWER

Recorded by
DUFFY POWER
on Fontana H. 230.

2/- NET

Youngstar Music Ltd
37-39 Oxford Street London W.1
Sole Selling Agents:
SOUTHERN MUSIC PUBLISHING CO. Ltd.
8, Denmark St., London, W.C.2

169

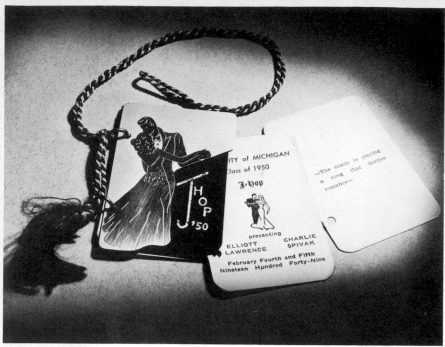

Dance-card, University of Michigan 'Hop', 1949

170

Cover of *Katy Keene*,
USA, 1958

PHILMAR

1200
PIECES
JIGSAW

SIZE 34″ × 23″

ʝ-saw puzzle, 1950s, showing escape from American forest fire.

Lid of American
lunch-box, 1950s,
showing teenagers
and motor scooters

about £30,000 a year. The Old Order might be symbolized by the University of Michigan Class of 1950 Hop, where each lucky girl guest was issued with a dance-card booklet with a design of an elegant couple dancing in evening dress on the metal cover, and inside, the slogan: 'The music is playing a song that invites romance.' And the New Order is represented by the pictorial gramophone record of Scott Wiseman's 'Time Will Tell' (also made in Michigan); by a skirt printed with rockers and screaming fans; by the songsheet 'Prettier Than You' featuring Duffy Power (one of the many young hopefuls who never quite made it); the 1956 remembrance service souvenir for James Dean, the moody leatherjacket who died in a car crash on America's Highway 466 that year; and a girl with a pony-tail on a motor scooter, that symbol of the new-found affluence of the young which was what gave them, for the first time in history, the power to choose what culture they wanted. Music was their chosen medium of revolt, as it had been of the upper-class Bright Young Things who jazzed away the Roaring Twenties. Those who did not choose to hurtle their bodies into the allegedly obscene rituals of jive, could sit at the side of the dance floor engaged in the dumb insolence of hand-jive, occasionally blowing pink iridescent bubbles of American gum. The characters of musical notation became motifs of decorative art at this time. They are shown here in a naïve but evocative drawing of 1957 by B. Hearn and in a headscarf design.

Although I am the same age as Cliff Richard, Tommy Steele, Adam Faith and John Lennon, I was not involved in the Rock Culture. I was a priggish, studious sixth-former, the archetypal 'swot', with exclusively classical and folksong tastes in music. I still cannot stomach the bawling type of rock, the boorish eardrum-beating insistence of 'Rock around the Clock' or 'Hound Dog', though I enjoy songs like 'When', 'Tell Laura I Love

Jive scene by B. Hearn, incorporating 'musical notation' motif, signed and dated 1957

Skirt with rock 'n' roll motif. English, 1956-59

Her', 'Runaway', 'Hit the Road, Jack', 'Dream Lover', 'Why Must I be a Teenager in Love?', Presley's wistful 'Girl of My Best Friend', the melancholy ballads of Roy Orbison, and 'Poetry in Motion' (of which, when I first heard it, I thought the beginning was 'O, a tree in motion'). But looking back now, with the something like enchantment which distance lends the view, I can see that rock helped to release us from the coyness, whimsy, prudery and twee of the early fifties. The so-called Angry young Men – who were not in fact dramatically young at the time[16] – were trying to do the same; but they were intellectuals, in most cases already too sold on or to the old culture to engender a new one. These men were about twice as old as the teenage rebels who were, in Thom Gunn's phrase, turning revolt into a style. They stood for things like 'common decency' (by no means a bad thing to stand for). They were not, like the intellectual leaders of the French Revolution, demagogues to inspire *enragés*. There was simply no point of contact between them and the *enragés*. When, in the sixties and seventies, the intellectuals did embrace the rock culture, it was like Marie Antoinette's shepherdess charades, or like learned Jacobin lawyers affecting *sans culotte* fashions. Marx thought that history always repeated itself, once as tragedy, then as farce. But what does farce repeat itself as?

Glazed terracotta model: Girl with pony tail, mounted on motor scooter, German, 1950s. Height 11.5 cm (4½ in.)

Silk headscarf incorporating 'musical notation' motif, 1950s

THE BEST OF AUSTERITY/BINGE

When this book was more than half-completed, Sir Paul Reilly, Director of the Design Centre, visited me to look at the illustrations I had so far mustered. Sir Paul is a genial and indulgent man, but I could feel his lack of enthusiasm mounting as we waded through the photographs. Eventually he exploded: 'But these are all the things that people who cared about design *hated*!' Why, he asked, did I not borrow from him photographs of the Design Council-approved works shown at the 'Britain Can Make It' exhibition of 1946 – the show which brought quarter-mile queues to the Victoria and Albert Museum to see how austerity could be palliated, if not beaten.

The trouble is, there is so much that is very worthy in Austerity/Binge design, but impressive only considering the conditions in which it was designed and made. Worthiness was the keynote of the 1946 exhibition. Early in their progress through the show visitors were introduced to its central theme, industry's swift and successful switch-over from war to peace. The show opened with 'an ingenious scene showing some of the British-made war equipment which helped to finish off Germany'. Exhibits were spotlighted by miniature searchlights shining through a partial blackout. Then gloom was replaced by brilliant lights to symbolize the transition to peace, and a shop-window presentation of the newest designs in small commodities. Housewives goggled at the

Poster issued by the Council of Industrial Design in the 1940s. Michael Pick

electric stoves with high-level ovens 'to obviate stooping' (whatever happened to those ?). 'Ironing', warbled *Photo World* of October 1946, 'can be a pleasure with the thermostatically-controlled electric irons which can be pre-set to give the correct heat for each type of material being pressed.' They were also fitted with 'a device to prevent the flex tangling in knots, handles designed to avoid wrist strain, grooved sole-plates to ease the tricky work of ironing under buttons, and double thumb-rests which give left-handed ironers a break'. All jolly sensible, very worthy; the Council of Industrial Design thought of everything. Housewives who had sacrificed their frying-pans to make into Spitfires found their virtue rewarded: a process originally invented to lengthen the life of Spitfire exhaust stubs had been applied to the manufacture of saucepans, and as a result it was claimed that the saucepans could be left to simmer for almost any length of time without the enamel cracking. There was a pair of household steps that turned into an ironing board *or* a baby's high chair; and carpet-sweepers that ran on a central track instead of wheels – and lots of other 'domestic doodahs' as *Photo World* put it, in plastic, now becoming socially acceptable. A portable radio set in the shape of a woman's handbag owed its origins to the valves used in the small radar sets incorporated in ack-ack shells and in bombs, and to the miniature radio sets dropped to members of the Resistance movements in occupied countries. Even a fabric golf bag had to be described as 'easily handled'. School, it was optimistically suggested, would become more popular with artificial fluorescent lighting emitting pink, blue and white beams, and a yellow 'blackboard' on which blue chalk was used 'to combine an effect of legibility and restfulness'. As for the children's section, that was 'like a pre-war grotto in a big store'. War production had resulted in the adaptation of many new ideas for the making of toys, most of which were turned out by men who a short time ago were making aircraft components. There were 'constructional housing sets complete with real mortar; dolls' houses equipped with an electric lighting system; baby jeeps and cast aluminium scooters for the child driver; perfect working models of tractors; miniature carpet sweepers'. One is reminded of Saki's short story 'The Toys of Peace', making fun of the 'peace toys' proposed by the Peace Council at the Children's Welfare Exhibition at Olympia after the First World War: in Saki's story, the toys of peace – models of a municipal dustbin, a municipal wash-house, a sanitary inspector, a wheelbarrow, a sewer ventilator and a school of art – were quickly converted by the children into instruments of war.

The Council of Industrial Design (founded 1946) was a quintessentially Herbivorous institution, a 'Take it from Here' body discreetly bullying the public into accepting their criteria of design. A 1940s poster issued by them shows the unengaging process in action; and, even allowing for the exigencies of Austerity, one cannot say much for their choice.

If it was functionalism you wanted, they ordered things better in America, away from the Cotswoldy arts-and-crafts influence of men like Gordon Russell. There the quest for the space-saving, the collapsible, the nestling, folding, and knock-down was in full career. The production of cheap and reliable plywoods, blockwoods and laminated boards in the inter-war period had already revolutionized methods of furniture manufacture. These new materials offered an alternative to the traditional frame-and-panel type of construction, one more suited to mass-production. Most plywood was produced in flat sheets, but the veneers could be glued up in curved shapes. Already before the war the Finnish architect Alvar Aalto had begun a series of experiments to make furniture entirely from bent plywood, resulting in the 'Finbar' range of furniture of the late thirties, in which the wood used was mainly Finnish birch: 'the chairs', Gordon Logie has written, 'became in effect one large spring which flexed downwards when sat on'.[1] Upholstery changed too: the old method of making a chair or bed soft, by a grid of steel springs overlaid with padding, was replaced by cast sponge rubber, especially in Italy.

The main exponent of the new furniture in America was the brilliant Charles Eames. There was an aerodynamic sharpness and cleanness of line to his designs which even the best of the British designers, men such as Robin Day and Clive Latimer, could not rival. In 1947 the Museum of Modern Art announced an international competition for low-cost

furniture. The judges included Mies van der Rohe, Gordon Russell, Réné d'Harnoncourt and Edgar Kaufmann, and the results, announced in 1950, give a good conspectus of furniture design at the meridian of our period. The first prize of 5,000 dollars for a seating unit (i.e. chair) was split between Don R. Knorr of San Francisco and Georg Leowald of Berlin-Frohnau. Knorr's seat, manufactured by Knoll Associates, New York, was of flat sheet metal bent round 'to meet itself in a seam in the form of a chair' – like a cone of paper with the pointed end snipped off. Leowald's design was of a continuous seat and back of moulded plastic sliding in metal grooves. Eames came second with a moulded fibreglass chair made by the Herman Miller Furniture Company, Zeeland, Michigan. This was a development of the laminated plywood chairs made with Eero Saarinen which had won the Organic Design prize of 1940. The co-winner of the second prize was Davis J. Pratt of Chicago, who attempted to solve the difficult problem of creating a *comfortable* modern chair by the use of an inflated tube perched on cocktail-cherry legs: the retail price was estimated at $30. The third prize went to Alexey Brodovitch of New York City for a clever knock-down design (i.e. you could take it to bits for packing) of a chair made of two vertical panels joined with lengths of plastic-covered resilient cord as seat. Honourable Mention in the 'seating unit' class went to John B. McMorran and John O. Merrill Jr of the Massachusetts Institute of Technology, for an ingenious if rather cranky chair which had a 'lounge position', a 'dining position' and a 'storage and shipping' position. The first prize in the storage units section went to Robin Day and Clive Latimer for a complex of cupboards and chests-of-drawers manufacturered by the Johnson-Carper Furniture Co. of Roanoake, Virginia. It had 'peaceful, horizontal lines' and recessed handles. Honourable mention went to Ernest Race of London for a neat 1950ish wardrobe.[2]

But far more important than any of these, to my mind, was the Italian school of designers led by Carlo Mollino. Because he was a pioneer and an innovator, Mollino, like Jean Puiforcat, the Art Deco silver designer, sometimes makes absurd and disastrous mistakes.

Console table and chair by Enrico Rava, Italy, 1948

He goes too far. But, as Puiforcat is to Art Deco, so is Mollino to Austerity/Binge: the genius of the style who crystallizes it in its most perfect form. It is the furniture made by him and his followers that the Madame Sonnabends and Alain Lesieutres will be selling, and Sotheby's, Belgravia, too, before long. I can best describe their collective style as 'streamlined surrealism'. Leonardo Borgese, writing in 1949 after a Milan exhibition of their work, described them in more flowery terms:

I must praise Franco Albini's fine line and his fourteenth-century sense of proportion. Also Paolo Buffa's rather English style with that firm, flexible line, like Gainsborough's women or a piece of Chippendale. Franco Buzzi's simplicity has an aristocratic warmth; I feel something grand and rustic in his rooms. I would like Gian Case to work on an open villa by the sea. I do not know how to praise Pietro Chiesa. (He is dead now. I hope there will be a whole book on him . . . .) Mollino has produced a modern tubular fantasy; one that makes one think now of medieval Nuremberg, now of the witches in *Macbeth*, now of fabulous birds and affable dinosaurs. . . . Renzo Mongiardino, a furnisher for the ladies of *Uncle Tom's Cabin*. . . . And Pippo Pestalozza? His furniture stretches out with the harmonious grace of a Botticelli youth. . . . Carlo Enrico Rava is a humanist, a refined technician, a rare calculator of rhythms and curves. Nino Repetto a classicist. And Sottsass junior, a florist, who wants to see us all sitting on his huge violets and his watchful pansies with their subtle, curved, flexible stems. And the fake fields of Fede Cheti, browsed by stone goats. Here we are going into Surrealism. Forgive me.[3]

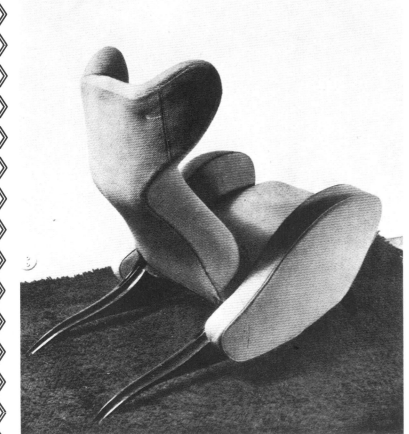

Upholstered reclining easy chair designed by Carlo Mollino and made by Cellerino of Turin, 1949, with Mollino's original design for the chair

178

Glass table designed by Carlo Mollino and made by Appelli and Varesio, Italy, 1949. The wooden side members are linked by metal strain rods

Table by Enrico Rava, Italy, 1949

A rather surrealist piece of writing. But Borgese did express very well the problems that beset most Austerity/Binge designers:

> Don't think that I don't know your suffering in this terrible, arid, inflated, destructive age. My friends, I know how tired you must be. You have to be purists and functionalists; you have to be modern; you have to be both artists and engineers; you have to be both cheap and expensive; you have to be plebeian and aristocratic; you have to have a modern style, and this modern style is difficult: it is line alone, form alone, subject alone, technique alone. . . . You must be original, you must be strict technicians and you must all be equal. You must follow fantasy and at the same time wretched rules. At least painters and sculptors have an art with a content and a subject. If they are willing, they are able; it is not something they cannot do even if they want to. Writers too have a definite form in the story. But you! You have to, you must, renounce the past, the old, the tradition. I understand. I sympathise with you.[4]

In silverwork there was no such originality to be found. Most silversmiths came to an uneasy compromise between traditionalism and Art Deco. A good example of this is the rose-bowl which Aubrey H. L. Gibson of Australia commissioned from R. E. Stone of Garrick Street, London, and with which he was so delighted that he wrote an entire book about it (*The Rose Bowl*, Angus & Robertson, London and New Zealand 1952). Stone is an admirable craftsman: the form is elegant, and the engraving (incorporating the palette motif) most competent. Yet no one would have been surprised to be offered this piece by Asprey's in 1932. It is a Jensen-like piece. An exhibition of Modern Silver at Goldsmith's Hall in 1954 showed the work of R. G. Baxendale, A. G. S. Benney, E. G. Clements, Francis Cooper, R. Y. Goodden, M. E. Gould, Reginald H. Hill, Geoffrey Holden, Stanley Morris, Philip Popham, C. J. Sniner, J. E. Stapley, R. E. Stone and A. G. Styles. None of them rose above the Deco-traditionalism mixture, and as some of them were still showing off their talents in 'rosewater dishes' this was hardly surprising: a vessel more appropriate to an Eastern prince's harem than to the drab-suited patrons of Austerity/Binge. Designers such as Leslie Durbin and Porteous Wood of Asprey's showed a pleasingly whimsical turn of design, but this could not be the basis of a new style such as Puiforcat, Templier and Sandoz had established in pre-war France.

Chelsea pottery photographed at the Chelsea studios in the 1950s by Sidney Bishop

Silver rosebowl made for Aubrey H. L.
Gibson by R. E. Stone, 1951

Porcelain coffee-service, decorated in
black and gold. Mark: a crown with
'Bavaria. Johann Seltmann. Vohen-
strauss'. Height of coffee-pot 17 cm
(6¾ in.)

Probably the real trouble was that there were just not enough people either with the money or willing to spend it on luxuries such as specially designed silver. The less intrinsically valuable arts certainly developed more impressively in the forties and fifties: ceramics (in which I would single out the wares of the Chelsea Pottery, founded by David Rawnsley), textiles (for example, Ben Rose hand-printed fabrics or the crisp design of Kenneth Rowntree for Edinburgh Weavers); plastics (interesting table lamps, radio sets, telly-trays, photo-frames, handbags and even the charming rattle by Robert Gutmann, which any Dum and Dee might quarrel over); glass (here the leaders were Sweden with Orrefors and Johansfors and Steuben, USA); and above all, graphics, especially book design by Bawden, Henrion, Barnett Freedman, Victor Reinganum and Hans Tisdall.

In the Austerity/Binge period, art was still a wicked luxury; Aubrey Gibson's literary gloat over his R. E. Stone rosebowl shows how lucky men considered themselves if they, were able to commission and obtain works of art. Art was almost on the ration. 'Multiples', 'disposables' and the Age of Warhol were far in the future.

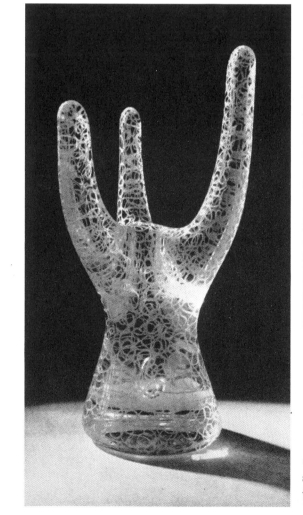

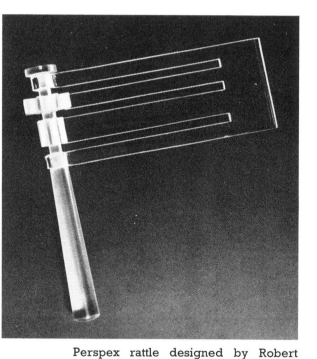

Perspex rattle designed by Robert Gutmann of Design Research Unit for ICI, 1949

'Vegetal Form' crystal sculpture designed by Bengt Orup and made by A. B. Johansfors, Glasbruk, Sweden, 1957. Height 18 cm (7 in.)

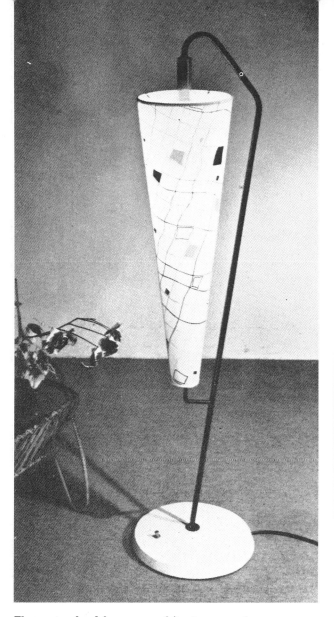

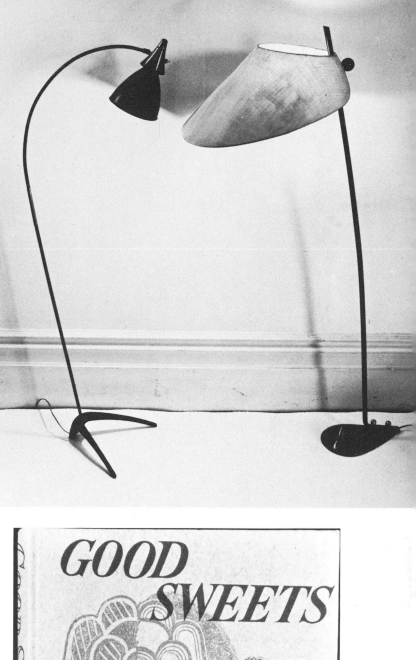

Floor standard lamp on white terrazzo base with foot-operated switch, and black and yellow patterned shade with perspex top diffuser. Designed and made by Troughton & Young (Lighting) Ltd, 1958. Height 132 cm (52 in.)

Top Right
1950s standard lamps. Dougie Field

Cover design by Edward Bawden for *Good Sweets* by Ambrose Heath, 1947

The Austerity/Binge revival

Borrowing from the past in the decorative arts has ceased to be mere plagiarism; it has now become grand larceny. First the Art Nouveau revival, then the Art Deco, and now Austerity/Binge, with the Beatle Culture of the early sixties not far ahead as well as not far behind. Though we may hope that a new, original style will be forged before long, we should not be too dispirited by the present cribbing from the past. After all, look what happened in the nineteenth century: a positive pageant of revivals, only finally ended by Art Nouveau, cubism and Art Deco: the Classical Revival, the Gothic Revival, the Tudor Revival, the Renaissance Revival, the Celtic Revival, the Queen Anne Revival, and the Rococo Revival.

So revivalism is nothing new, and I am confident that eventually a new original style will again be thrown up. There was, as they say, no good dramatist in England between Sheridan and Wilde. But in the late 1960s it seemed reasonable to predict that a twenties/thirties revival would be succeeded by a forties/fifties one – if only in quest of new material for commercial exploitation by fashion designers, record companies and stage writers. I decided I would chronicle this revival, when it arrived, stage by stage.

The revival was dashingly launched by a special issue of *Design* magazine, January 1970, to celebrate their twenty-first anniversary (1949–1970). The issue had a splendid fold-out cover pastiching both the forties and the seventies, by Bentley, Farrell and Burnett, the young designers who had been so active in the Deco revival (and who have now gone their separate ways, in true pop-group style). The first article in the issue was 'Mid 40s: back to the drawing board' ('After five years' rude interruption post-war designers picked up where they had left off. But a new style was beginning to emerge.') Sir Hugh Casson contributed a piece on the 'Britain Can Make It' exhibition of 1946. The third article was on 'Late 40s: messages' ('The New English style prospered and unity was fought for'). Further articles dealt admirably with the Festival of Britain, concentrating on the Battersea Pleasure Gardens, the Coronation, 'Early 50s: mixed blessings', and '55–65: mainstream evolution'. I am full of admiration for this issue of *Design*: within the compass of a magazine it would hardly be possible to cover the period better.

An article in the London *Sunday Times* of 27 September 1970 describes the beginning of the Austerity/Binge revival in fashion and lifestyle:

> At the Black Raven pub in Bishopsgate, on Friday and Sunday nights, it's as if the 1960s had never been. The bar is filled with men, most of them around the age of 30, wearing the classic costume of the historic Teddy Boys: drapes, crêpes and bootlace ties. Deafening music from the juke-box insists on the simple beat of early rock 'n' roll. The dancing preserves the athletic tradition of American jive. A chance client might think that some time machine had transported him 15 years back into the past. But the proprietor, Bob Acland, would assure him that he had stepped into the immediate future.

Bob Acland was right. In 1971, forties fashions in dress took over from Deco ones. The *Sunday Times* of 21 February carried an article entitled 'Paris: back to the pin-ups of the forties'. The September issue of *Honey* led with 'New Look Forties Fashion for the Autumn': 'Points to watch for are huge exaggerated shoulder pads, extra-wide lapels, nipped-in waists. . . .' The *International Times* of 26 August-September 9 had a satirical cover of a voluptuous forties pin-up in provocative pose, with the caption '– and they call hippies obscene. . . .'

By October the forties revival had hit America. *Esquire* in that month produced an issue with a Petty Girl swinging nudely across the fold-out cover, which bore the caption: 'Welcome back to the 40's: the last time America was happy.' O those happy happy Forties, of rationing, Pearl Harbor and Bundles for Britain. Inside was a photograph of Andy Warhol in forties zoot suit with reat pleat, and a grotesquely silly article by George Frazier: 'What was very odd was the wartime of the Forties – tinkling with laughter; touched by massive dignity, and yet with no one demeaned and outraged by any awareness of needless slaughter.' Tell that to Belsen survivors. Or, for that matter, to the marines.

Mr Frazier told Americans what they might be nostalgic about. The murder of the Philadelphia baseball player Eddie Waitkus – 'rather a lark'. The Roosevelt funeral train winding its way north from Georgia while sobbing Negroes lined the tracks. Frank Sinatra. Bogart. Erroll Flynn ('a Forties' person') and statutory rape – 'a serious charge yet in the Forties as funny as a barrel of monkeys'. Lauren Bacall. Jane Russell. Betty Grable's gams. Jitterbugging. The Lindy Hop. Sweater girls. Ankle straps. Paramount News. Bugsy Siegel full of bullets. Ernie Pyle writing for the home folk about the boys at the front. Oh yes, it was terribly amusing to be alive in the USA of the 1940s.

Cover of *IT*, 26 August – 9 September 1971

Chelsea Set; the Hon. Emma Tennant as debutante; a photograph taken by Anthony Armstrong-Jones before he married Princess Margaret

Fold-out cover of *Esquire* October 1971,
with 'Petty Girl'

Coca-cola advertisement from the
Washington Post, 19 April 1973

A series of records reviving popular song-tunes of the 1940s. 1972

The lead article in *Seventeen* ('Young America's Favorite Magazine') of November 1971 was 'Jive to the Look of the 40s'. The December 1971 issue of the *Illustrated London News* carried a cinema review by Michael Billington headed 'Faithful to the '40s'. He suggested that after the big musicals based on *The Sound of Music*, after the motor-bike movies that followed *Easy Rider* and the protest films and soft-focus studies of revolution such as *Getting Off* and *The Strawberry Statement*, 'all the signs indicate a return to the traditional genres, in particular the laconic, sharp-edged, '40s style thriller'. He was speaking of *The Last Run*, directed by Richard Fleischer and starring George C. Scott, and of *Klute* – 'another film that harks back to the 1940s'; and what he had to say might apply equally to *Gumshoe*. Later films which more directly capitalized on the forties revival were *Summer of 42* and its paler sequel *Class of 44*, and *Carnal Knowledge*, or the splendid wartime romance between Glenda Jackson and Brian Deacon in *The Triple Echo*. In 1971 too was published Alan G. Barbour's *A Thousand and One Nights* subtitled 'An affectionate pictorial history of those fantastic films of the 40s, with fond recollections of the best

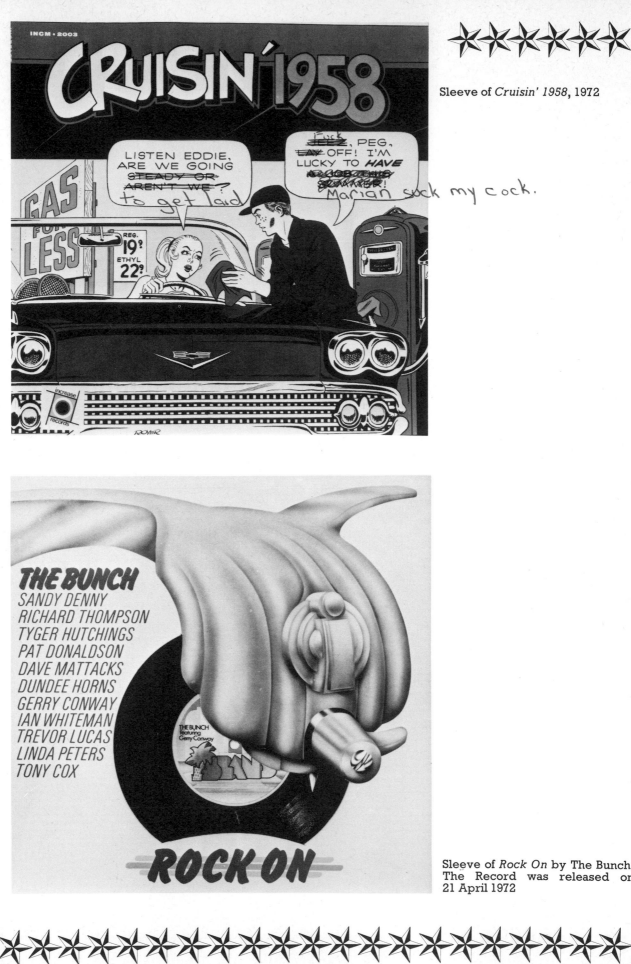

Sleeve of *Cruisin' 1958*, 1972

Sleeve of *Rock On* by The Bunch.
The Record was released on
21 April 1972

Saturday afternoon serials'. The cover picture and several of the illustrations inside were from the overpoweringly kitsch film *Cobra Woman* (Universal, 1944), starring Maria Montez as the evil queen of Cobra Island. Charles Higham's and Joel Greenberg's *Hollywood in the Forties* had already been published in 1968; in 1971 Gordon Gow's *Hollywood in the Fifties* followed. Alan Thompson's *The Day Before Yesterday* ('An illustrated history of Britain from Attlee to Macmillan' based on a 1970 television series) also appeared in 1971. This had worthy predecessors, in no way tied to a nostalgic revival of the forties and fifties, but rather crowing over their graves – *The New Look, a Social History of the Forties and Fifties* by Harry Hopkins (Secker & Warburg, 1963) and *The Fifties* by John Montgomery (Allen & Unwin, London; Fernhill House, New York, 1965).

The Evening Standard (London) of 26 January 1972, covered its centre spread with articles about the revival in Teddy-boy costume – knee-length jackets, drainpipe trousers, winkle-pickers, bootlace ties and D.A. haircuts[1] – and recorded the opening of a new rock revival shop in the Kings Road, Chelsea, called 'Let it rock'. There was no doubt that 1972 was going to be the year of the Fifties Revival, and in the *Evening Standard* of 4 March Ray Connolly devoted his column to explaining why. 'The Fascinating Fifties' it was headed: 'Ray Connolly on the Whys and Wherefores of London's Newest Cult'. Connolly began by quoting from the top of the pops of the moment, 'American Pie', a song dedicated to Buddy Holly, which contained the lines:

> Long, long time ago, I can still remember
> How that music used to make me smile . . . .

The lyric was supposed to be a brief history of pop and its development during the previous fifteen years, 'while at the same time containing a welling yearning for the more simplified days of the 'fifties. Connolly added: 'That it should have caused such a stir at this particular moment is not surprising, because, more and more, 1972 looks like being the year that the 'fifties and all the cult heroes associated with that period again become high fashion.' He listed the portents: *The Last Picture Show* (Bogdanovich) was opening in London in a week's time – about growing up in a small Texas town in the fifties; Broadway had come up with *Grease,* a musical parody of the rock 'n' roll, slicked-back hair era, including such songs as 'Look at Me, I'm Sandra Dee', 'Shakin' at the High School Hop', 'Born to Hand Jive' and 'It's Rainin' on Prom Night'. Rick Nelson had just revisited England 'and killed his long-time image by trying to look and sound progressive (at a time when he should have been cashing in on his old-time following)' and Chuck Berry was coming back later in the spring – 'At least one can be sure that he won't have changed'.

Connolly's explanation of the fifties revival is so interesting that I have obtained his permission to quote it at length:

> The youth culture that blossomed in the mid- to late fifties, first in the United States and then in Europe, was a direct result of a suddenly increased affluence, and the maturing of a new generation of young people uncowed by the traumas of unemployment, war and rationing that had always threatened their parents.
> With rapidly expanding economics (during a period of peace under the paternalistic panache of Macmillan and Eisenhower) a new market was found in the young and relatively well-off, and to fill the demand a new culture began to be formed – with its own screen heroes like James Dean and Marlon Brando, and in a rather different style Marilyn Monroe, and on record by people like Buddy Holly, Elvis, and the rest.
> There had been idols before, of course, and Sinatra was the biggest. But he was also, in his way, the biggest fraud, since the emotions and people he sang about bore little relation to emotions and people as they really existed. His was a never-never land of romance. The new stars were singing about love that sounded a lot like lust.
> Some people feel nostalgic for the war, the blitz and the social cameraderie encouraged by the difficulties of the duration, but the awful carnage of those years also made a lot of people want to forget. The post-war years were drab and difficult, and

it wasn't in fact until well into the mid-fifties that new and individual styles began to develop of themselves.

Suddenly young people were being called teenagers, and instead of looking like younger versions of adults, they took on a life style of their own. A new social style was evolving which was to mushroom extraordinarily during the next decade.

In Britain, however, we seemed to come to teenage second-hand. The heroes of the 'fifties were all American (only Americans could play rock and roll) and we virtually lived in a fantasy world of trying to marry the lyrics to American records with our own society. We heard songs about high-school hops, and proms, and graduation, and drive-ins – but it was all a never-never land which we couldn't hope to really emulate in Britain. Before the Beatles we were living out an alien culture.

Connolly went on to make the point that in the fifties, the drugstore, the candy bar, hamburger joints and even Levi jeans, were things we only heard about on records or saw in films. But now, in the post-Beatle period, we were at last assimilating them into our lives as fact, not fantasy: witness the Drugstore in Chelsea, hamburger bars like the Great American Disaster, and the vast number of boutiques.

But secondhand though it may have been, the 'fifties era did have a quaint charm. In a much more regimented and conformist society the number of daily decisions facing every one were that much fewer, and some of the major problems of today were remote and well hidden. It's a self-deception, of course, but life did seem considerably easier then from a moral point of view. . . . I sometimes think that the trouble with today is that there's no need to wake up Little Susie: she's been awake all the time.

The London 'alternative' magazine *Time Out* of 21–27 April had a well-drawn cover showing Jerry Lee Lewis in an expresso bar with juke box. Inside was a photograph of Lewis 'as he looks now at the Palladium on Sunday'; a long list of Rock clubs in the London suburbs; a review of some 'legendary masters' records including Fats Domino's 'The Fat Man' (1949) which 'more or less invented rock 'n' roll', Eddie Cochran, Ricky

Nelson, a collection called 'Rock 'n' Roll is Here to Stay'; and an announcement that *To Have and Have Not* (Bogart/Bacall, 1944) was on at the Electric Cinema Club. Inside the back cover was an advertisement for the record 'Rock On' by the Bunch, which was released on 21 April. Other revival records issued in 1972 were 'Roxy Music', 'Cruisin' 1958' (and other fifties years) and a series of medley records of the war years, issued in the United States by London.

The Daily Mirror (London) of 30 May 1972 represented both the Austerity and Binge revivals in three articles. One, headed 'Dad's Army Falls Out', described how the last Home Guard outfit in Britain had decided to call it a day, having met weekly since the official disbandment of the Home Guard in 1945. Side by side with a photograph of the real veterans of the Home Guard was printed a clip from the successful British television series 'Dad's Army', an affectionate satire of Home Guard antics introduced each week by Bud Flanagan's crackly rendering of a pastiche song in Second World War style, called ''Oo do you think you are kiddin', Mister Hitler?' The second article, by Benny Green, was headed 'Forward – Into the Fifties!'

> As the decade opened, Bernard Shaw fell out of a fruit tree in his ninety-fifth year and finally left the world to its own devices. Winston Churchill, a mere 76, was on the brink of a triumphant return to power. There was still some rationing, still a few shortages. All over the country the immaculate hair of Denis Compton gleamed down from the Brylcreem hoardings. . . . Above all there was Suez, at which point the British realised it had been a long time since Mafeking and that it might be as well to admit it. And perhaps there lies the clue.
>
> The 1950s were the last decade of the comfortable old notions about Empire, Chastity, Morality, Education, Patriotism – a last fling for all those sacred cows to be so relentlessly hunted down in the 1960s and finally laid to rest in the 1970s. . . . There were debs and no detergents, virginity and no abortion, at least not officially, no stereo, no deodorants for men.

And the third article, by Michael Hellicar, gave the by now familiar low-down on Malcolm McLaren's new shop 'Let It Rock', where the brocade waistcoats, drape jackets, bootlace ties, crêpe-soled shoes and drainies were still selling strongly, and a one-man attempt was being made to revive the Brylcreem industry.

Hellicar described the life of the typical Teddy Boy: 'A Ted lived for Saturday night. He'd spend two or three hours putting on all the gear, looking just right. Then he'd swagger down to the local palais and spend the next few hours dancing and parading in front of all his mates.' That was for the proles, but the fifties were still a highly class-oriented time, and *Harper's and Queen* of May 1972 had as its main article a piece by Gloria Gladstone on 'The Chelsea Set – 15 Years On'. The label 'Chelsea Set' was invented by the *Daily Express* gossip columnist William Hickey 'to cover the goings-on of anyone, whether they lived in Chelsea or not, who seemed to have the friends and freedom of manner that could be served up in tomorrow's social column as an alternative to the predictable names and events of the London Season'. The Chelsea of 1956 'had remained unmapped almost since the day Oscar Wilde eloped from Tite Street. An SW10 postmark still wore the air of delivery in a cleft stick by native runner'. It was put on the map, apparently, by people like the raffish Mark Sykes, Simon Hodgson ('famous for cheques'), Mary Quant and Alexander Plunket-Greene with their 'Bazaar', 'Dandy Kim' Waterfield, Emma Tennant, Ian Dunlop and Lady Jane Vane-Tempest-Stewart. Their headquarters were the Markham Arms and the misspelt Fantasie coffee bar. The Chelsea Set, Miss Gladstone thought, 'marked the end of fifteen years of war and austerity'; and, casting many a wistful look behind, she concluded:

> With the decline of the Beatles and the odd behaviour of footballers, the public will shortly need fresh heroes. It is difficult to see where these are to come from unless the old totems of titled identity and the grace that sometimes goes with it are dug up once again from where they were buried in the Kings Road years ago.

Teddy Boys and Chelsea Set: these were distinctively British contributions to the fifties, at a time when most of our culture or lifestyle were, as Connolly says, 'second-hand'. But what of the American lifestyle we tried to imitate, or adopted wholesale? On 16 June 1972, *Life* magazine gave over most of an issue to 'The 50s – wacky revival of Hula hoops, Duck-tails, Sock hops, Marilyn Monroe look, Rock 'n' roll and Elvis'. The article was called 'The Nifty Fifties':

> It's been barely a dozen years since the '50s ended and yet here we are again, awash in the trappings of that sunnier time, paying new attention to the old artifacts and demigods. Elvis Presley, back from exile in the movies, gave his first Madison Square Garden concert last week. Kids barely old enough to remember what a fall-out shelter was are digging the hand jive and the Bunny Hop, circle skirts and cinch belts, penny loafers, saddle shoes, white bucks and shirts with cigarette packs tucked into rolled-up sleeves. Disc jockeys pump out Golden Oldies by Bill Haley, Chuck Berry and Little Richard. Sock hops are big on campus and at neighborhood bistros where mommas and poppas pushing 30 can hear 'Who put the bop in the bop sh-bop sh-bop, who put the ram in the ram-a-lam-a-ding-dong?' and say 'They're playing our song.' Thanks in part to *Grease,* a lively Chicago-born put-on of the '50s rock 'n' roll scene that muscled its way on to Broadway, the Marilyn Look is back and so is the Greaser Look, shiny-shirted, with ducktail hairdos molded into a Vaseline aspic. Pop psycho-logists – and many of the kids – see the flight to the '50s as a search for a happier time, before drugs, Vietnam and assassination. Dick Biondi, a Chicago DJ, thinks it might even end the generation gap.

The picture section that followed featured the Sha-Na-Na, a Columbia University group who plastered their long hair with a tube of water-soluble grease apiece 'and do more than 200 oleaginous concerts a year' and had spawned imitators such as Flash Cadillac and the Continental Kids, from Boulder, Colorado. Sha-Na-Na, whose name came from the nonsense syllables of 'Get a Job' (1958) was born when Columbia choristers made a hit singing '50s numbers at the 1967 Ivy League trivia championships. The picture feature also included the young stars of *Grease*, Carole Demas and Barry Bostwick (aged twenty-six). One fifteen-year-old girl summed up the appeal of the show for her: 'Those greasers were the first freaks.'

The musical revival reached its climax in Britain on 5 August 1972, when a Rock 'n' roll Festival was held at Wembley Football Stadium near London. The *Evening Standard* devoted a special colour issue to it, containing an interview with Chuck Berry, an article on Jerry Lee Lewis, '14 years after the scandal that almost wrecked his career' (he had married a thirteen-year-old girl), and an interview with Little Richard, a revivalist in more than one sense, who incanted at the end of the interview: 'Like the Bible says, ''Them that wait on the Lord, He shall renew their strength''.'

The Rock Festival (described by the London *Evening Standard* as 'the biggest Teddy Boys' picnic ever') was front-page news in the following day's *Observer*. Some 50,000 people had attended to listen to Chuck Berry, Billy Fury, Bill Haley, Jerry Lee Lewis, Screaming Lord Sutch and Little Richard, who, 'heavily made up for the occasion, attacked his piano and screamed about Black Power. He took off some of his clothes and threw them to the crowd. But the crowd first slow-handclapped him, then booed him off.'

In sober contrast to this jamboree, a long article appeared in the *Times Literary Supplement* five days later on 'The Fifties and their followers', about an exhibition of Dutch poetry, 1949-55, being held at the Dutch Literary Museum and Documentation Centre in The Hague. The poetry of such men as J. Bernlef and K. Schippers, it appeared, shared two characteristics with other artistic and cultural movements in Europe of the time – a 'total renewal' and a 'romantic' cast. It is perhaps not surprising that recovery from the war – 'regeneration' – was happening in the Netherlands at roughly the same time as in Britain and other European countries; the Dutch, it is true, had more to recover from (in that Holland had been occupied), but correspondingly, no doubt, more passion to recover.

Two pages from *Town Markets* advertising magazine, London 1972

The issue of *Honey* for September 1972 spread itself with a lively and slightly sardonic Rock 'n' roll supplement, the stars (including the very minor British ones) deftly dismissed with a single tag : Chuck Berry : sharp, and slick and evil ; Little Richard : wildest, campest, insanest, greatest of them all ; Pat Boone : positively radiant with purity ; Paul Anka : flashy, greasy, extremely precocious . . . and so on through Bobby Vee, Del Shannon, Gene Vincent, Wee Willy Harris and the rest.

The ostentatiously luxurious fashion magazine *L'exclusif* (Paris and Milan) paraded a thoroughly Austerity/Binge wardrobe in its 1972 summer issue. This kind of fashion was percolating downwards, too, so that the grisly first issue of *Town Markets* magazine, basically a London advertising rag, carried a double-page spread, badly enough designed to seem almost correctly in period, of '40's Combat' and '50's Expresso' clothes – mixing up the hairstyles, clothes and accessories of just about every decade from the beginning of the twentieth century with happy abandon.

1972 was also the year of Granada TV's grand exercise in nostalgia, *A Family at War* ; of George Nobbs's book *The Wireless Stars* (Wensum Books, London), 'a Cat's Whisker touching the crystal of the memory', recalling Tommy Handley, Arthur Askey, Richard Murdoch, Henry Hall, Vera Lynn, Lord Haw-Haw (William Joyce), Wilfred Pickles, Ben Lyon and Bebe Daniels, Dick Barton – Special Agent, Donald Peers, Peter Brough and Archie Andrews, Tony Hancock and the Goons. In America, John Mebane's *Collecting Nostalgia* ('The first guide to the antiques of the 30s and 40s') was published, a book drawing mainly, but interestingly, on old trade catalogues. Mickey Mousery seemed to be the staple of the American revival market. The *Hampstead and Highgate Express* of 17 November recorded that Terence Rattigan's wartime hit *While the Sun Shines* was to be performed as part of the Hampstead Theatre Club's Christmas programme. The play was first produced in 1943. 'And an added attraction will be a foyer display of 1940s memorabilia – ration books, old newspapers, wartime posters and photographs and even gas masks, if they can be found.'

American nostalgic party invitation, August 1973, Keith Marshall

remember the 50's?

when you could be a ~~cool~~ *Fog* ~~cat~~ without smoking dope or talking dirty in front of the chicks

relive those bland old days!!

rob pitcher's 2109 decatur august 4 sat. 9:00 — till··· ···endsville

By 1973 the Austerity/Binge revival had become too widespread to chronicle minutely; '*passim*' is the appropriate word. But deserving special mention is Simon Jenkins's facetious article 'The return of the foggy fifties' in the *Evening Standard* of 2 January:

> The 'fifties revival has definitely come to stay. On Saturday I drew back the curtains and there it was – a good old-fashioned London fog.
> Like most revivals, it wasn't quite the real thing. It was a bit cleaner and fresher and was decidedly short of the familiar sulphurous sooty particles. It therefore lacked the full authentic yellowish hue of the true early 'fifties pea-souper. Connoisseurs might have called it a country fog rather than a London smog.

Also the 19 April advertisement for Coca-Cola in *The Washington Post* telling us, rather belatedly, that the pin-ups now 'are dressing up for a super summer of '73 in dresses straight out of the Forties!' Or the magazine *Custom Car* for March, with its 'Remember the Fifties!!' feature and cover design. Or the *Standard* again on 30 July, telling men to get rid of their long hair and take 'four steps to a fifties short cut'. *Grease* was now on in London, and films such as *That'll Be the Day* and *Let the Good Times Roll* were causing boys to reach for the scissors and Brylcreem. Ann Carpenter wrote in the 30 July *Standard* that 'Down at Crimpers in Baker Street, men are walking into the salon at the rate of several a week and demanding their crowning glory be shorn and shaped into the fifties style of yesteryear.'

An auction of Forties clothes and of Italian furniture by designers such as Mollino was held in Milan. The *Rocky Horror Show* – an amusing send-up of fifties rock music, horror films ('I am Doctor Frankenfurter') and general fifties' camp – moved triumphantly from theatre to theatre up the Kings Road, Chelsea. Dealers such as Digby Howard, Michael and Linda Costiff and Susan Marsh, all in the Kings Road, sold forties and fifties accessories, as did the shop called 'Magazine' at 444 Third Avenue, New York, and more than one shop in Greenwich Village. The Arts Council, London, held its 'Decade '40' exhibition of painting, sculpture and drawing in Britain, 1940–49. Fifties rock parties took over from 'Roarin' Twenties' ones. The French relived their own most fierce and graphic forties memories – of women collaborators being shorn and painted with swastikas after the Liberation – through the sarcastic pages of the satirical magazine *Hara Kiri*.

194

The Rock Revival was fed by the Radio One *Story of Pop*, an encyclopaedia in 26 weekly parts, and by several books: Steve Prope's *Those Oldies But Goodies: a Guide to 50s Record Collecting*; Ian Whitcomb's *After the Ball*; Siegfried Schmidt-Joos's *Rock Lexikon*; Guy Peellaert's and Nik Cohn's *Rock Dreams,* a slightly sinister rendition of Rock mythology in words and pictures and Graham Wood's *An A-Z of Rock and Roll.* No one lived out Rock myths more wholehoggingly than the artist Dougie Field, who not only painted oils of fifties subjects, but ripped up a good fitted carpet in his Earl's Court, London, flat, to lay down some polka-dot linoleum, and sold a superb Art Deco bed because he wanted to commission another for himself in the form of a palette.

With the fuel economies and petrol rationing caused by the oil shortage after the Arab-Israel War, there was a new welling-up of nostalgia for those simple, happy, authoritarian days of the forties. Hunter Davies contributed a nice ironic article to the *Sunday Times* of 2 December 1973 about queuing for petrol coupons:

> Gosh, yesterday was so exciting. I was at the post office long before opening time, hoping there would be a simply enormous queue and I would be able to hear some sparkling cockney repartee as we all suffered together and put our backs to the wall and smiled and whistled and showed Jerry what we were made of. I'd hoped there might even be a few all nighters, sleeping on the pavements, their gas masks at the ready, sharing out the Spam sandwiches . . . .
>
> They were such lovely times, weren't they? There were no strikes in those days. No hijacking, no pornography, no towns full of foreigners, no pollution, no Common Market, no violence, no raping, no mugging, no people running down the country, no jokes about the Union Jack. We were all so much happier then, weren't we? We never had any homosexuals during the war.
>
> I really do think dried egg tasted much nicer than fresh eggs. And as for dried milk, that was yummy. Corned beef is now an expensive delicacy, but in those days, everyone had it. I remember the terrible disappointment, just after the war, when I tasted my first banana. I must have been about 10 and I was playing football in the park when I heard this cry a long way away: 'The Co-op's got Bananas.' As it got nearer, I joined in and hundreds of us rushed through the streets, shouting: 'The Co-op's got Bananas.' They didn't taste a patch on the mashed parsnips which my mother had been giving us for afters all through the war, telling us it was exactly the same taste as bananas.

And Hunter Davies concluded: 'I feel sorry for kids today. They're deprived of being deprived.'

Dougie Field in his 1950s revival flat in Earls Court, London 1972

Notes

Introduction

1 *Art Deco of the 1920s and 1930s* Studio Vista, London; Dutton, New York 1968, and *The World of Art Deco* Studio Vista, London; Dutton, New York; The Minneapolis Institute of Arts, 1971.
2 'And in which events I had a small share.'

The Arts of War

1 See Denis Judd *Posters of the Second World War,* Wayland, London 1972.
2 I stand open to correction by bibliophiles, but the earliest photographic jacket I have seen is on *Memories of Bygone Eton* (1907) by Henry S. Salt, bearing a sepia photographic portrait of the author. Graphics-only jackets predominated up to the end of the 1950s; only in the 1960s did the photographic jacket take precedence.
3 Mollie Panter-Downes told readers of the *New Yorker:* 'Since every citizen has been forbidden to stir a yard from home without his or her gas mask, public ingenuity has occupied itself . . . with the problem of how to carry the by now familiar cardboard container. A neat canvas case worn slung from the shoulder makes the whole thing as innocuous as a Kodak, and is popular with the men. It has been observed that Queen Elizabeth, on her numerous smiling visits to the various women's organizations in London, carries her gas mask this way.' (Reprinted in *London War Notes* 1939-1945, Longman, London 1972, p.8.)
   A further despatch recorded the existence of 'gas masks for dolls complete in smart cases. Children's gas-mask cases are now available, too – jolly affairs that soften the whole sorry business with coloured pictures of Donald Duck and Bo-Peep. It is said that the new masks for children under five are to be pastel-tinted so that the dreary functional design may not obtrude too horrifically against some tender nursery colour scheme' (*ibid.,* p.23).
4 See the 1969 Arts Council of Great Britain catalogue of the *Deutsche Akademie der Kunste* exhibition 'John Heartfield, 1891-1968, photomontages'.
5 See B. Hillier *The World of Art Deco* Studio Vista, London; Dutton, New York; Minneapolis Institute of Arts, 1971; pp. 192-3.
6 This subject is covered in detail in my forthcoming book *Bad Taste.* But those interested may seek the origins of 'Nazi' style in sculpture in the work of Hermann Prell (see Adolf Rosenberg *Prell* Leipzig 1901) and of Reinhold Begas (see Alfred Meyer

Reinhold Begas Leipzig 1901) and Franz Metzner (see Otto Stoetzl *Franz Metzner* Prague 1905); and will find examples of Nazi statuary and painting in *Kunst Dem Volk* Munich 1939-43 and *Signal* Paris 1941-43. A good article on Arno Breker appeared in the *Sunday Times* colour magazine, London, 7 November 1971.
7 From *Paper and Print,* vol. 18 London 1945, p.99; quoted by Mark Gabor *The Pin-up: a Modest History* Deutsch, London 1972, p.77.
8 Reprinted in Mollie Panter-Downes *London War Notes, 1939-1945* Longman, London 1972, p.43.
9 See John Harman, 'Oliver Messel builds a world of fantasy', *John Bull,* 28 August 1954, p.17: 'During the war, as a captain in charge of a camouflage unit, he was billeted in an eighteenth-century house in Norwich. Finding that the house, which was of great architectural value, was suffering from years of neglect, Messel restored the original decorations. ''It was probably the only building in Britain which was improved by army occupation.'' '
10 'Not for nothing was James Gardner Chief Development Officer for Army Camouflage during the war: in ''Britain Can Make It'' he camouflaged austerity. He made a post-war fantasy.' Fiona MacCarthy, *All Things Bright and Beautiful* Allen & Unwin, London 1972, p.146.
11 See John Lewis, 'The Wood-Engravings of Blair Hughes-Stanton', *Image* 6, Spring 1951, p.43: 'At the outbreak of war Hughes-Stanton was commissioned in the Royal Engineers, and became a camouflage officer. He served in the Middle East and went to Greece. At the end of that ill-fated expedition he was captured. Whilst in a prison cage he was shot through the jaw by a trigger-happy German sentry. By some miracle he was not killed, and after a prolonged progress through various military hospitals, he was eventually repatriated. Whilst in prison hospitals he did some moving and interesting drawings of patients.'
12 See Geoffrey Barkas, *The Camouflage Story,* Cassell, London 1952, pp.45-6: 'Hughes-Stanton was new to me. He was not very large or robust, but he was manifestly keen and easily taken to. He had dark, unruly hair and dark eyes. When he laughed, which he did freely, his face puckered up, his eyes almost disappeared, and he seemed to inhale his laughter. From the others I learnt that he was a well-known engraver and artist in wood-cut. I noticed his hands – capable, unusual hands, apparently double-jointed in all fingers.'

13 William Fagg *Divine Kingship in Africa* British Museum booklet, 1970, p.20.

The Post-War Temper

1 See Flight-Lieutenant Edward Hall, RAF, 'The Solace of Richard Jefferies', in *Richard Jefferies: A Tribute by Various Writers* ed. Samuel J. Looker, 1946:
'And then came the call – France, immediately – September, 1939. My country had need of me, at long last. There was a meandering trickle through a flower-strewn meadow, midway between Verdun and Metz, where I sought and communed once again with Jefferies . . .
'Another call – this time the Middle East – Egypt, Palestine, Syria and back again to Egypt – and forsaking noisy, dirty, clamorous Cairo, with my back turned to the green strip of the Nile and its insignificant Pyramids, I stood in silent prayer, looking towards the Suez over a vast desert of calcined mountains, through which twined sandy empty river-beds, and again I was with Jefferies – he of the green fields, but also of the perfect downs – he who had found God against a sky-scape, from a bed of sweet-smelling thyme . . .' A footnote adds: 'Flight-Lieut. Hall carried Looker's *Jefferies' England* everywhere with him on his travels to the East and back again.'
2 These were among the books on the subject published in the forties and fifties: 1944 L.T.C. Rolt *Narrow Boat;* 1945 Frank Eyre and Charles Hadfield, *English Rivers and Canals;* 1947 Emma Smith *Maiden's Trip,* Brian Waters *Severn Tide,* Susan Woolfitt *Idle Woman,* William Bliss *Canoeing* (2nd edn, 1st edn, 1934); 1948 Montague and Ann Lloyd *Through England's Waterways,* Susan Woolfitt *Escape to Adventure;* 1949 Brian Waters *Severn Stream;* 1950 N. Carrington and P. Cavendish *Camping by Water,* L.A. Edwards *The Inland Waterways of Great Britain,* Charles Hadfield *British Canals,* Eric de Maré *The Canals of England,* John O'Connor *Canals, Barges and People,* L.T.C. Rolt *Inland Waterways of England;* 1951 L.T.C. Rolt *The Thames from Mouth to Source;* 1955 Robert Aickman *Know Your Waterways,* Robert Aickman *The Story of Our Inland Waterways,* Charles Hadfield *Introducing Canals,* Charles Hadfield *The Canals of Southern England;* 1958 L.T.C. Rolt *Inland Waterways;* 1961 L.T.C. Rolt *Waterway.*
3 On wood-engraving of the forties and fifties see: John Farleigh *Graven Image, an Autobiographical Textbook*

(1940); George E. Mackley *Wood Engraving* (1948); Thomas Balston *English Wood Engraving, 1900-1950* (1951); Dorothea Braby *The Way of Wood Engraving* (1953); Wilfred Gregson *A Student's Guide to Wood Engraving* (1953); Mark F. Severin *Your Wood Engraving* (1953); John Farleigh *Engraved on Wood* (1954); John Biggs *Wood-cuts, Wood Engravings etc.* (1958); *The Wood Engravings of Robert Gibbings* (1900); and Ruari McLean *The Wood Engravings of Joan Hassall* (1960). The fifth issue of *Image* magazine (Autumn 1950) was devoted to Balston's survey of wood engravers. *Image* also published the following articles on individual wood-engravers: Stuart Rose, 'The Wood Engravings of John O'Connor' (Summer 1949); Thomas Balston, 'The Wood-Engravings of Ethelbert White' (Winter 1949-50); Richard Gainsborough, 'The Wood-Engravings of Buckland-Wright' (Spring 1950); John Lewis, 'The Wood-Engravings of Blair Hughes-Stanton' (Spring 1951); Thomas Balston, 'The Wood-Engravings of George Mackley' (Summer 1952).

4 See Peyton Skipwith, 'Recalling Ethelbert White', *The Connoisseur*, March 1973, vol 185, no. 745 for an illustration of the caravan.

5 See Lord Birkenhead, '*F.E.*,' 1960

6 'Last spring (1947) when I was wandering aimlessly about the outskirts of Barcelona, I came across a camp of Gypsy Coppersmiths. They belonged to the tribe of Cristo-jordi, many of whose members I had met in my travels through Spain and Africa in former years. These coppersmiths had wandered from country to country during the six years of war and their passports, which they proudly showed me, had been guaranteed by the International Red Cross. The chief of the tribe narrated his adventures in the drawling voice of chante-fable: they were mainly accounts of frenzied flights from police and Gestapo, and agonizing quests for food. As a primitive Gypsy, he thought of the World as a spacious garden full of fine, fat hedgehogs; ''The Lord will provide'' was his motto, for He feedeth the Gypsies as He doth the birds of the air; but all this harmony is destroyed by War. War is the product of the ''Beng'' or devil and quadruple team of apocalyptic horsemen; a series of cataclysms that descends upon the World, leaving it as parched as the desert.' W. Starkie *Raggle-Taggle: Adventures with a Fiddle in Hungary and Roumania* Murray, London 1949.

7 Louis MacNeice *Collected Poems 1925-48* Faber & Faber, London 1949, p.211.

8 Walter de la Mare *The Burning Glass* Faber & Faber, London 1945, p.31.

9 These include: 1942 Enid Blyton *Circus Days Again,* M. Willson Disher *Fairs, Circuses and Music Halls*; 1946 Sir H. G. Tyrwhitt-Drake *The English Circus and Fairground*; 1947 *At the Circus,* anon., Raphael Tuck, Gertrude Keir *The Circus,* Marjorie Norton *Circus Lady*; 1948 Rupert Croft-Cooke (ed.) *The Circus Book,* Lady Eleanor Smith and John Hinde *British Circus Life, Circus Thrills* Juvenile Productions; 1949 C. G. Finney *The Circus of Dr Lao,* Mary Cathcart Borer and Cecil Musk *Circus Boy* (Book of the film by Patita Nicholson, 1949), Enid Blyton *Circus Book*; 1950 Baroness Maisie de Kerchove *Circus poodles and Other Rhymes*; 1951 Rupert Croft-Cooke *The Circus Has No Home,* Muriel Levy *Le Cirque. Les aventures de pouf, trans.* Anne-Marie Menantean; 1952 *The Circus Book,* anon. Publicity Productions, J. Y. Henderson *Circus Doctor* as told to Richard Taplinger, Pixie Gann *The Circus Game,* Warren Penn *Circus in the Attic,* Enid Blyton *The Circus of Adventure*; 1953 James Hemming *Circus Visitors*; 1954 Mary Grant Bruce *Circus Ring, The Circus (follow the dots),* anon., Ward Lock, *Circus Painting Book,* anon., Blackie; 1955 I. Knight *The Circus Comes to Town,* C. V. Jackson *Circus Twins*; 1956 *Circus,* anon., Picture Books, Dora Broome *Circus Pony,* Joan Selby-Lowndes *Circus Train,* Gladys Emerson Cook *Circus Clowns on Parade,* Christian Staub *The Circus*; 1957 *The Circus to Town,* anon., Ladybird Children's Book, Joan Selby-Lowndes *The First Circus: The Life of Philip Astley.*

10 Jon Akass, 'Pass the gum, chum, and let's all go celebrating', *The Sun* 20 December 1971, p.6.

11 In his forties poem 'The Mermaid', Charles Madge wrote:
As ripple, beam, zephyr, a smiling sight,
Steered past his Needles, turned the winking buoy,
His siren blows 'Home'. Mirror and comb delight
Her tranquil now. Spent is the waves' annoy.

12 Harry Hopkins, writing of Christmas 1945 (*The New Look* Secker & Warburg, London 1963, pp.42-3) says: 'The more desperate parents combed the second-hand shops. A pair of roller-skates (prewar value 3s. 1d.) was bid up to £3 in an auction; for ladies a roll of parachute silk (two coupons) was understood to be highly acceptable.'

13 See also Frank Davis, 'A Mermaid out of Water', *Country Life* 9 March 1972, p.572. Plate I of this article shows Delvaux's *La Sirène* of 1950 of which Mr Davis writes: 'The poor girl resembles a wet fish on a slab, and I do not admire wet fish on slabs – no wonder she is so pensive . . . .' This drawing, in pen and Indian ink and watercolour, had just fetched £9,200 at Sotheby's.

14 These are illustrated, on pp.24 and 23 respectively, of *Decorative Art, 1951-52* Studio, London.

15 *Photoplay* May 1957, p.16. ('On a bed of strawberry and velvet, Debra Page husks: ''Do I excite you ?''').

16 1946 Eileen Molony *The Mermaid of Zennor; and other Cornish Tales*; 1947 Maureen Pretyman *The Mermaid of Kilshannig*; 1949 Barbara Leonie Picard *The Mermaid and the Simpleton*; 1955 Douglas Shepherd *The Mermaid and the Matador*; 1956 Eva Boros *The Mermaids*; 1957 Richard Carrington *Mermaids and Mastodons*; 1958 Charmian Clift *Mermaid Singing,* J. Bowen *The Mermaid and the Boy*; 1959 Stratis Myrivilis *The Mermaid Madonna.*

17 On Ruthven Todd, see the amusing chapter titled 'Calder-Marshall and the Reverend Todd' in J. Maclaren-Ross *Memoirs of the Forties* Secker & Warburg, London 1965, pp.109-17.

18 On analysis of fairy tales, see Maureen Duffy *The Erotic World of Faery,* Hodder & Stoughton, London 1972.

19 On the way in which the seaside resorts responded to the great demand for seaside holidays, see John Batten, 'Selling the Seaside', in *Contact* no. 11, 1948; and Eric Wainwright, 'Blackpool Spit and Polish', in *Leader* magazine, 27 May 1950. Holiday camps flourished in this period: see Stanley Baron and Frederic Mullally, 'Butlin Between Seasons', in *Contact* no. 10, 1947, pp.55-63; and *The Daily Mail Film Award Annual* 1947, pp.124-6 for an account of the film *Holiday Camp* (director Ken Annakin). And on an autobiographical note, I worked at Butlin's Holiday Camp, Skegness, in the summer of 1959, between school and university. A huge notice ran along the main façade: 'OUR INTENT IS ALL FOR YOUR DELIGHT.'

20 The advertisement is reproduced in *Modern Publicity 1951-52* Studio, London, p.77.

21 *ibid.* p.38.

22 *ibid.* p.106.

23 Reproduced in *Daily Mail Film Award Annual,* 1947.

24 Reproduced in *Decorative Art, 1943-48* Studio, London, p.ii.

25 Reproduced in *Modern Publicity, 1951-52* Studio, London, p.63.

26 *ibid.*

27 Reproduced in *Decorative Art, 1953-54* Studio, London, p.83.

28 Reproduced in *Decorative Art, 1943-48* Studio, London, p.111.

29 Reproduced in *Decorative Art, 1949* Studio, London, p.80.

30 Reproduced in *Decorative Art, 1954-55* Studio, London, p.103.

31 On Grigson, see 'Deadly Rustic: the two Geoffrey Grigsons', *Times Literary Supplement,* London, 31 July 1969, pp.845-6.

32 *The End of an Age and Other Essays* Putnam, London 1948.

33 Quoted in Ulrich Conrads *Programmes and Manifestoes on 20th Century Architecture* Lund Humphries, London 1970; MIT Press, Cambridge, Mass, 1971, p.150.

34 *ibid.* p.157.

35 *loc. cit.*

36 One stanza of George Barker's 'Vision of England' ran:
Alone on the dark beach I stood.
The teeth of the seas tore the shore.
'O immensely sad land,' I said,
'where
Only the ghosts are good.'

37 See the frontispiece to his *Paper Sculpture* Blandford 1947.

38 The books on ballet which appeared between 1941 and 1948 are listed by Haskell in *Ballet Since 1939,* revised

197

edn, British Council/Longmans 1948, Appendix E.

39 This jacket is illustrated in B. Hillier, *Art Deco* Studio Vista, London; Dutton New York 1968, p.150, and in *The World of Art Deco* Studio Vista, London; Dutton, New York; Minneapolis Institute of Arts 1971, p.14.

40 Christopher Finch *The Art of Walt Disney* 1973, p.425.

41 Finch illustrates just such a camera in action, *op. cit.*, p.34. Claes Oldenburg expresses the same idea pictorially; see his 'Mouse head variations' in *Notes in Hand* Dutton, New York 1971.

The Fifties

1 See B. Hillier, *Art Deco* Studio Vista, London; Dutton, New York 1968, pp.88-9 and 93-4.

2 Gerard Hoffnung was born in Berlin in 1925 and came to London in 1939. His death in 1959 deprived the world of a cartoonist of genius, of a clown of the airwaves, an impresario and a dedicated musician with a passion for the brass. In his short life he produced thirteen books, seven of them about music, which have sold over half a million copies. He created a brand of symphonic caricature, the Hoffnung Music Festivals, in which parody and scholarship combined in one of the most professional serio-comic jokes to be found in the arts.

3 Quoted by Michael Frayn 'Festival', in M. Sissons and P. French (ed) *Age of Austerity* Hodder & Stoughton, London 1963. p.330.

4 She had already written *Fun Without Flowers, My Roses, 101 Ideas for Flower Arrangement, First Steps with Flowers* and *Floral Roundabout,* all published by C. A. Pearson, London.

5 Arno Schönberger and Halldor Soehner *The Age of Rococo* Thames & Hudson, London 1960, p.8.

6 Voltaire *Letters Concerning the English Nation* ed. Charles Whibley, 1926, p.98.

7 These included: 1950 Kenneth Heur *Men of Other Planets* London; 1952 Kenneth Arnold and Ray Palmer *The Coming of the Saucers* Amherst, Wisconsin; 1953 Desmond Leslie and George Adamski *Flying Saucers Have Landed* London; 1954 Cedric Allingham *Flying Saucers from Mars* London, Leonard G. Cramp *Space, Gravity and the Flying Saucer* London, Daniel W. Fry *The White Sands Incident* Los Angeles, Donald E. Keyhoe *Flying Saucers from Outer Space* London, Captain Howard James, 'We were shadowed from Outer Space' *Everybody's Weekly* London, 11 December 1954; 1955 George Adamski *Inside the Space Ships* New York, Waveney Girvan *Flying Saucers and Commonsense* London, Frank Scully *Behind the Flying Saucers* London, Dr H. Percy Wilkins *Flying Saucers on the Moon* London, *Flying Saucer Review* started in London. Sample article: Desmond Leslie, 'Mexican Taxi Driver meets Saucer Crew' (vol. 2 no. 2 March-April 1956); 1956 Gavin Gibbons *The Coming of the Space Ships* London, Aimé Michel *The Truth about Flying Saucers* New York, Edward J. Ruppelt *The Report on Unidentified Flying Objects* New York; 1957 Gavin Gibbons *They Rode in Space Ships* London, Donald E. Keyhoe *The Flying Saucer Conspiracy* New York, *Diario Illustrado*, Lisbon 16 November 1957; 1958 Aimé Michel *Flying Saucers and the Straight-Line Mystery* New York, *Correio da Manha* Rio de Janeiro, 21 February 1958; 1959 G. H. Williamson *Road in the Sky* London.

8 Dorothy Wellesley *Lost Planet and Other Poems* Hogarth Press, London, 1942, pp.18-19.

9 J. Bronowski, *The Ascent of Man* BBC, London 1973, pp.331-2.

10 On the development of television as medium, see the special issue of *The Twentieth Century,* November 1959.

11 The scale and scope of the exercise is well conveyed by John Montgomery in *The Fifties* Allen & Unwin, London 1965, pp.116-170.

12 *ibid*.

13 Michael Frayn, 'Festival' in *Age of Austerity,* ed. Michael Sissons and Philip French, Hodder & Stoughton, London; Verry, Lawrence, Mystic Conn. 1963, pp.319-20.

14 Waugh wrote in the epilogue to his novel *Unconditional Surrender:* 'In 1951, to celebrate the opening of a happier decade, the Government decreed a Festival. Monstrous constructions appeared on the south bank of the Thames, the foundation stone was solemnly laid for a National Theatre but there was little popular exuberance among the straitened people, and dollar-bearing tourists curtailed their visits and sped to the countries of the Continent where, however precarious their condition, they ordered things better.'

15 Thom Gunn, 'Elvis Presley', published in *The Sense of Movement* Faber & Faber, London 1957, p.31.

16 'John Braine was thirty-four, Kingsley Amis was thirty-two, and John Wain was twenty-eight when each published his first novel. All started later, not earlier, than usual. True John Osborne had a play running in London's West End when he was twenty-six, but none of the new rebels was really young.' (John Montgomery *op. cit.*, p.138).

The Best of Austerity/Binge

1 Gordon Logie *Furniture from Machines* Allen & Unwin, London 1948.

2 On the subject of the Museum of Modern Art competition, and for the biographies of individual designers, I am greatly indebted to Edgar Kaufmann's *Prize Designs for Modern Furniture,* New York 1950.

3 Leonardo Borgese, preface to Guglielmo Ulrich, *Arredatori Contemporanei,* Milan, 1949.

4 *op. cit.*

The Austerity/Binge revival

1 For readers too young to remember, or posterity: winkle-pickers were sharply pointed shoes; and D. A. stood for duck's arse, referring to the way the back of men's hair was swept back in two 'wings' meeting at a central vertical.

Index

199